Contents

AI-POWERED EDUCATION MARKETING: 100 WAYS TO ELEVATE YOUR SCHOOL'S BRAND

DR DHEERAJ MEHROTRA

Preface

*Friends, Education faces a critical moment in a technologically advanced age. As artificial intelligence transforms sectors worldwide, schools and educational institutions face new problems and opportunities. **"AI-Powered Education Marketing: 100 Ways to Elevate Your School's Brand"** is a comprehensive guide for educators, administrators, and marketing professionals who want to use AI to improve their school's outreach and brand.*

These pages contain handpicked methods that combine cutting-edge AI with proven marketing principles. The 100 techniques here offer unique ways to boost your school's visibility, attract top talent, and build essential community relationships, from personalised student recruiting efforts to data-driven decision-making tools.

We must embrace the instruments that will shape learning as we traverse modern education's complexity. This book shows how AI can transform education marketing and gives you the tools to implement these tactics.

If you're a tiny private school trying to boost

enrolment or a huge university looking to expand globally, this book will give you the tools and ideas to boost your institution's brand in the digital age.

Explore and innovate with AI-powered marketing to revolutionise your educational institution.

Author

www.authordheerajmehrotra.com

ONE

THE WAY FORWARD

The book "AI-Powered Education Marketing: Ways to Elevate Your School's Brand" is an indispensable resource in the current educational environment, which is saturated with competition.

This guide provides creative ways to improve a school's exposure, engagement, and enrolment using artificial intelligence (AI). When institutions fully use AI, they can personalise their marketing efforts, optimise resource allocation, and make data-based decisions.

These tools, which range from predictive analytics to automated content generation, allow educational institutions to communicate with the appropriate audience precisely when necessary.

In an era in which digital presence is of the utmost importance, this method assists educational institutions in standing out, establishing closer connections with potential students and parents, and ultimately thriving in an academic market rapidly increasing in complexity. Adopting artificial intelligence in education marketing is no longer a choice; it is necessary for future success.

1. Personalised Emails: AI can analyse parent preferences and send personalised emails to promote school activities and successes.

Sample Tool:

Personalized Emails: Mailchimp with AI integration

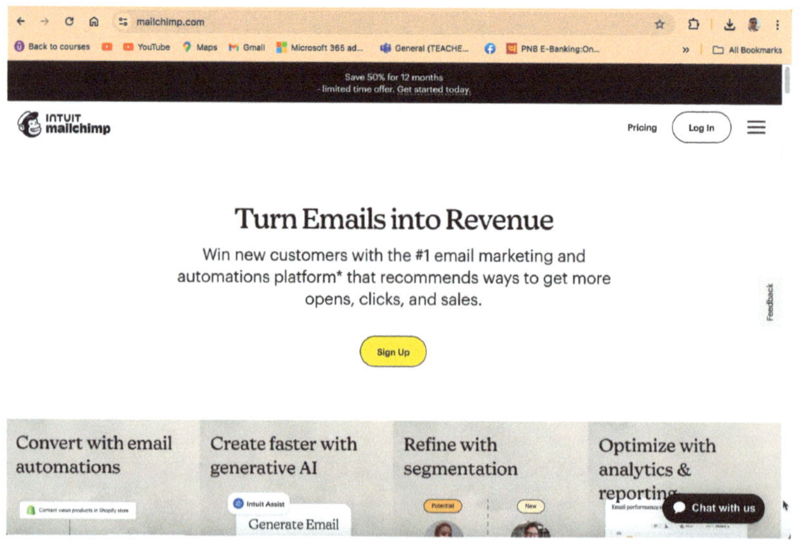
mailchimp.com
Back to courses
YouTube
Maps
Gmail
Microsoft 365 ad...
General (TEACHE...
PNB E-Banking:On...
All Bookmarks
Save 50% for 12 months
- limited time offer. Get started today.
INTUIT mailchimp
Pricing
Log In
Turn Emails into Revenue
Win new customers with the #1 email marketing and automations platform* that recommends ways to get more opens, clicks, and sales.
Sign Up
Feedback
Convert with email automations
Create faster with generative AI
Refine with segmentation
Optimize with analytics & reporting
Intuit Assist
Generate Email
Potential
New
Chat with us

www.mailchimp.com

2. Chatbots: Use AI-powered chatbots on the school's website to respond to potential parents' questions around the clock.

Sample Tool:

Chatbots: Intercom AI

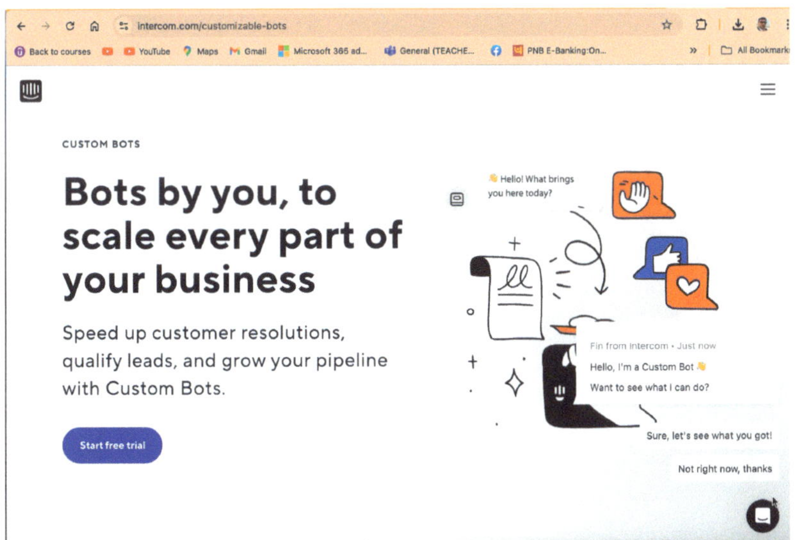
intercom.com/customizable-bots
Back to courses   YouTube   Maps   Gmail   Microsoft 365 ad...   General (TEACHE...   PNB E-Banking:On...   All Bookmarks
CUSTOM BOTS
Bots by you, to scale every part of your business
Speed up customer resolutions, qualify leads, and grow your pipeline with Custom Bots.
Start free trial
Hello! What brings you here today?
Fin from Intercom · Just now
Hello, I'm a Custom Bot
Want to see what I can do?
Sure, let's see what you got!
Not right now, thanks

www.intercom.com

3. Social Media Analytics: Use AI to monitor and analyse social media interactions and customise marketing plans.

Sample Tool:

Social Media Analytics: Sprout Social AI

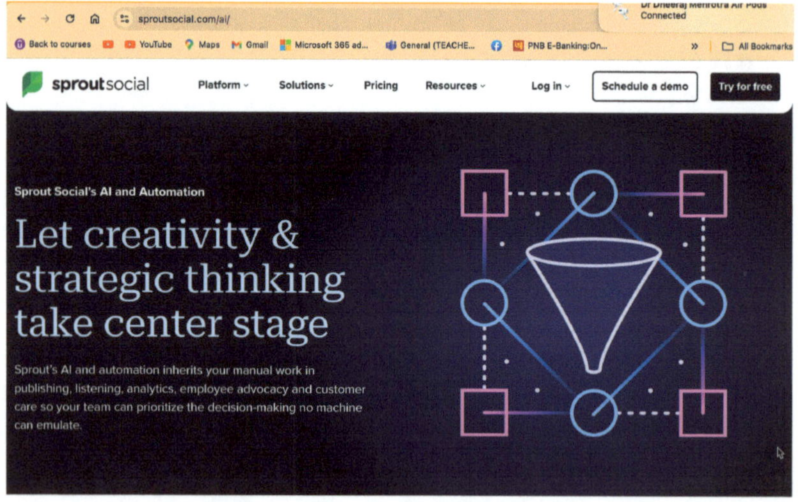
sproutsocial
Platform
Solutions
Pricing
Resources
Log in
Schedule a demo
Try for free
Sprout Social's AI and Automation
Let creativity &
strategic thinking
take center stage
Sprout's AI and automation inherits your manual work in publishing, listening, analytics, employee advocacy and customer care so your team can prioritize the decision-making no machine can emulate.

www.sproutsocial.com

4. Predictive Analytics: Position the school as a forward-thinking institution by forecasting educational trends and student demands.

Sample Tool:

Predictive Analytics: IBM Watson Analytics

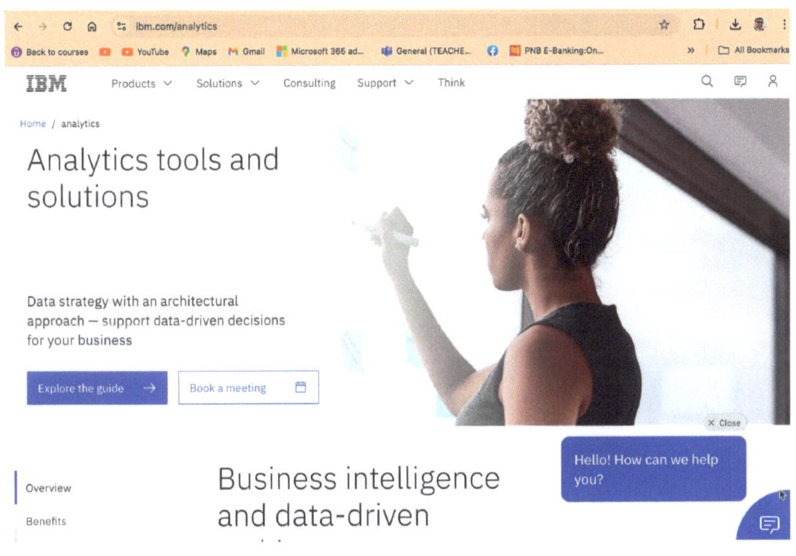

www.ibm.com/analytics

5. Targeted Advertising: Use AI to produce targeted adverts on social media platforms for specific demographics.

Sample Tool:

Targeted Advertising: Albert.ai

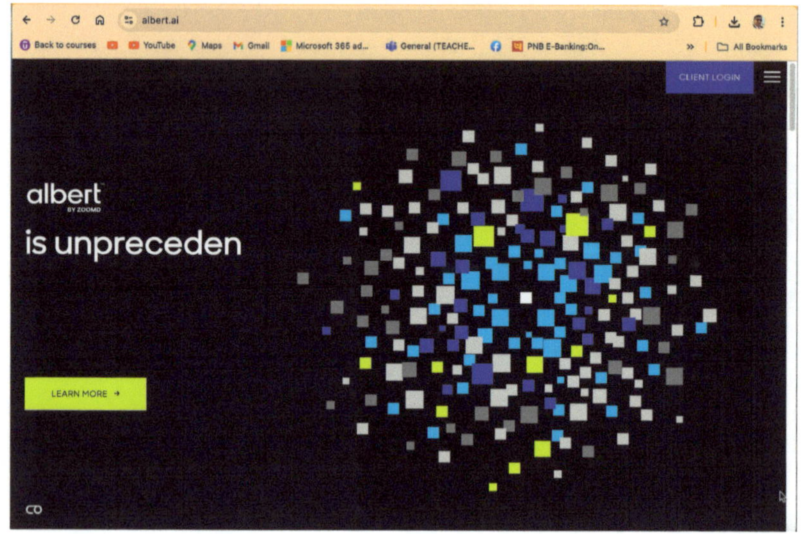

www.albert.ai

6. AI-Powered Content Creation: Create blogs, emails, and articles that appeal to parents and students.

Sample Tool:

AI-Powered Content Creation: Jasper.ai

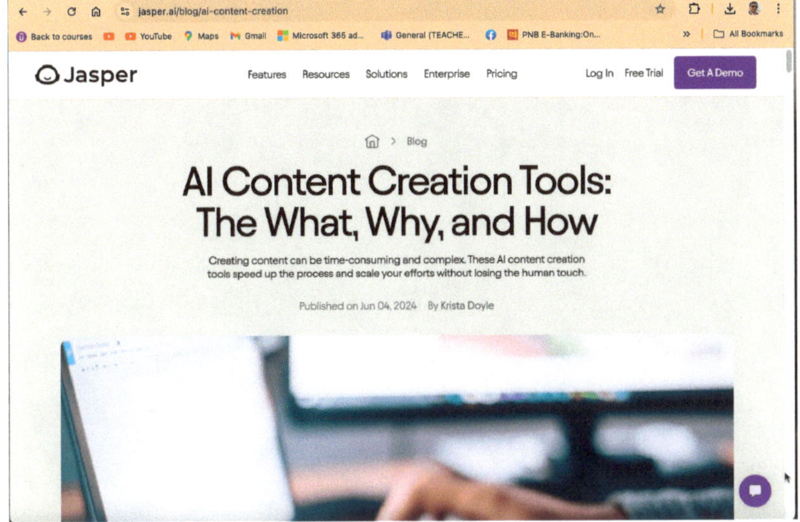

www.jasper.ai

7. Virtual Campus Tours: Create AI-powered virtual tours that provide tailored experiences depending on customer preferences.

Sample Tool:

Virtual Campus Tours: Matterport AI

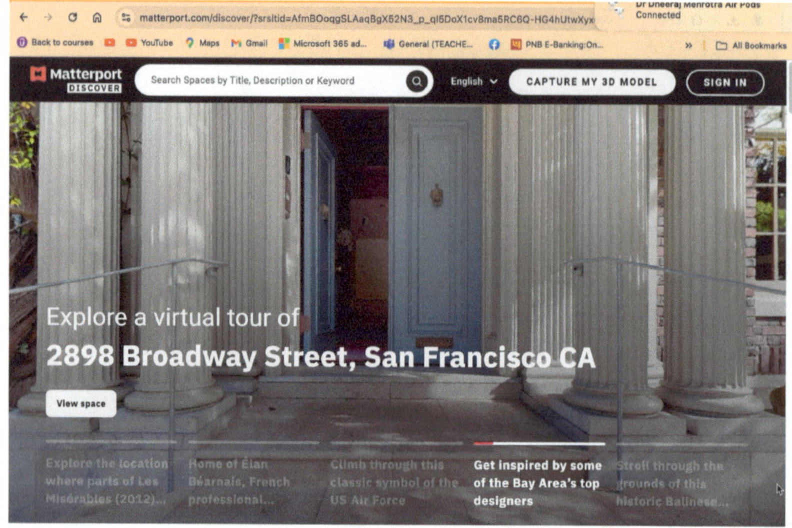
Matterport
DISCOVER
Search Spaces by Title, Description or Keyword
English
CAPTURE MY 3D MODEL
SIGN IN
Explore a virtual tour of
2898 Broadway Street, San Francisco CA
View space
Explore the location where parts of Les Misérables (2012)...
Home of Élan Béarnais, French professional...
Climb through this classic symbol of the US Air Force
Get inspired by some of the Bay Area's top designers
Stroll through the grounds of this historic Balinese...

www.matterport.com

8. Parent input Analysis: Using AI, analyse parent input and promote good testimonials in marketing materials.

Sample Tool:

Parent Input Analysis: Qualtrics XM with AI

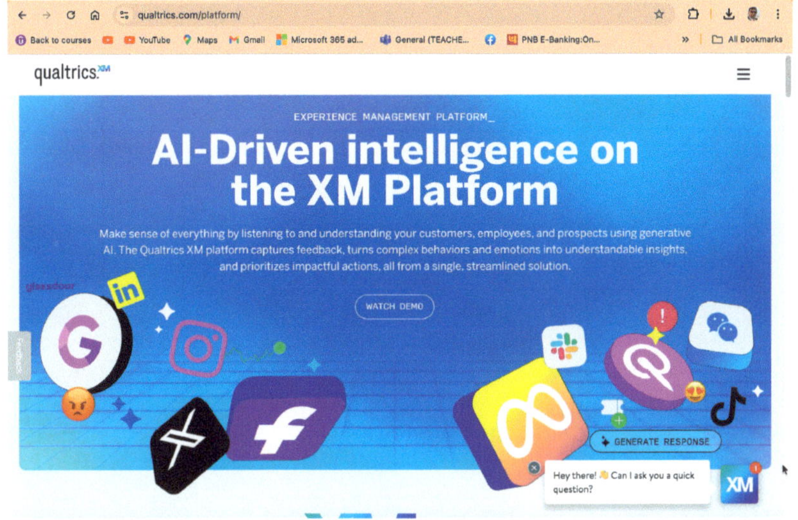
qualtrics.XM
EXPERIENCE MANAGEMENT PLATFORM_
AI-Driven intelligence on
the XM Platform
Make sense of everything by listening to and understanding your customers, employees, and prospects using generative
AI. The Qualtrics XM platform captures feedback, turns complex behaviors and emotions into understandable insights,
and prioritizes impactful actions, all from a single, streamlined solution.
WATCH DEMO
GENERATE RESPONSE
Hey there! Can I ask you a quick
question?
XM

www.qualtrics.com

9. Optimised Website SEO: Use AI techniques to improve the school website's search engine rankings.

Sample Tool:

Optimized Website SEO: SEMrush AI Writing Assistant

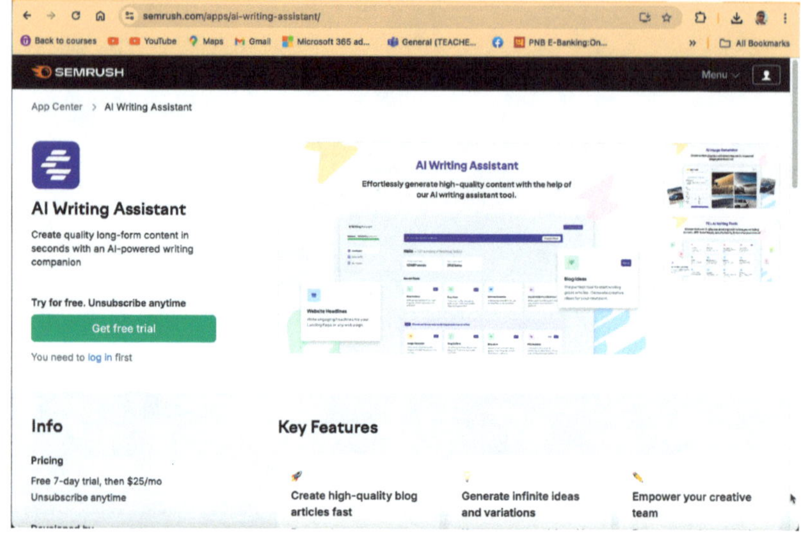

www.semrush.com

10. Video Marketing: Create AI-generated content highlighting school activities and triumphs.

Sample Tool:

Video Marketing: Lumen5

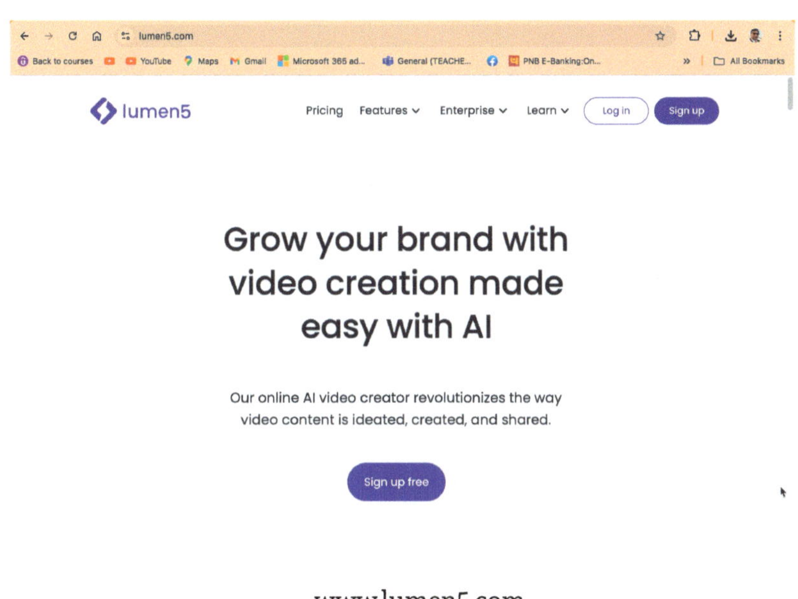

www.lumen5.com

11. AI-Driven questionnaires: Use AI to create and analyse questionnaires to obtain feedback from parents and students.

Sample Tool:

AI-Driven Questionnaires: SurveyMonkey AI

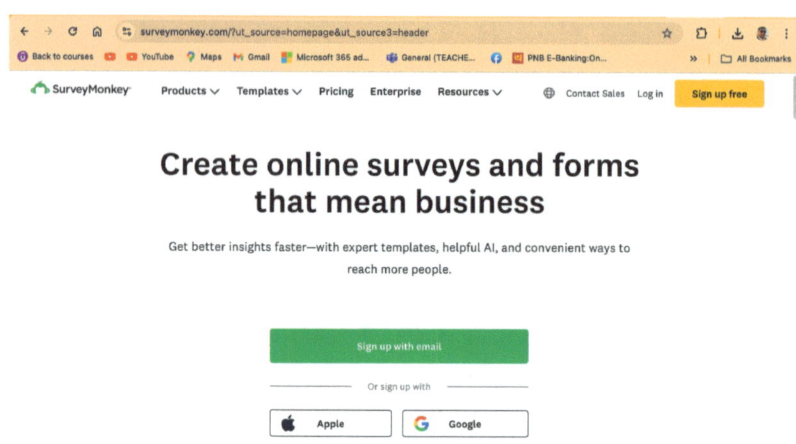
surveymonkey.com/?ut_source=homepage&ut_source3=header
Back to courses   YouTube   YouTube   Maps   Gmail   Microsoft 365 ad...   General (TEACHE...   PNB E-Banking:On...   All Bookmarks
SurveyMonkey   Products   Templates   Pricing   Enterprise   Resources   Contact Sales   Log in   Sign up free
Create online surveys and forms
that mean business
Get better insights faster—with expert templates, helpful AI, and convenient ways to
reach more people.
Sign up with email
Or sign up with
Apple   Google
Sign up free. No credit card required.

www.surveymonkey.com

12. Interactive FAQs: Use AI to create interactive FAQs for the school's website.

Sample Tool:

Interactive FAQs: Frase.io

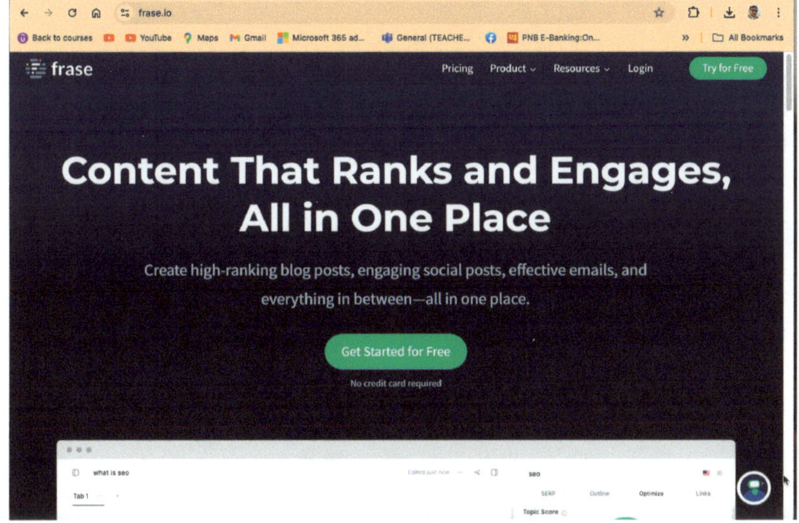

www.frase.io

13. Enrolment Predictions: AI can forecast enrolment patterns and assist in tailoring marketing campaigns accordingly.

Sample Tool:

Enrollment Predictions: Rapid Insight

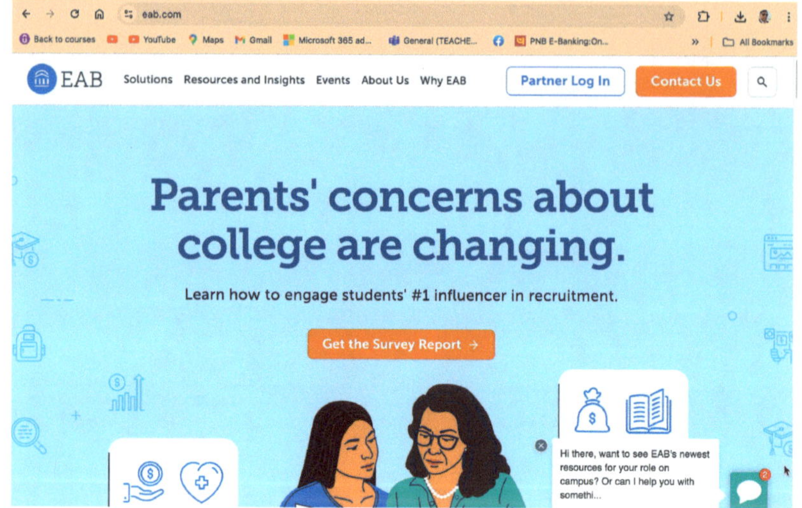
EAB
Solutions   Resources and Insights   Events   About Us   Why EAB
Partner Log In
Contact Us
Parents' concerns about college are changing.
Learn how to engage students' #1 influencer in recruitment.
Get the Survey Report →
Hi there, want to see EAB's newest resources for your role on campus? Or can I help you with somethi...

www.eab.com

14. Personalised Parent Portals: Use AI to improve the user experience and engagement.

Sample Tool:

Personalized Parent Portals: Blackbaud K-12 Solutions

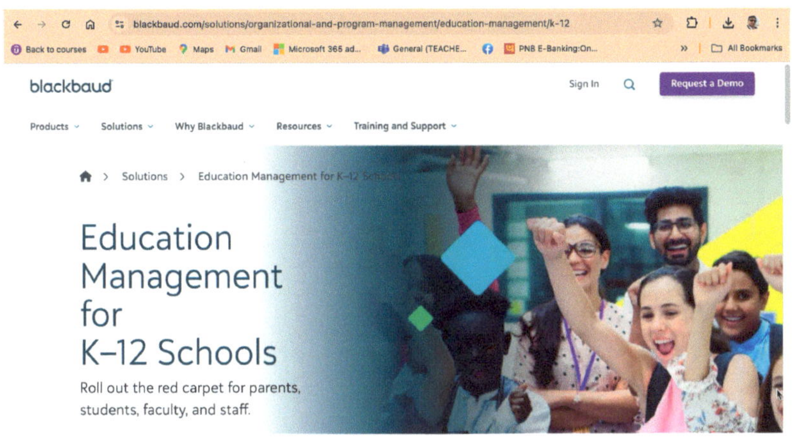

www.blackbaud.com

15. Automated Follow-Ups: Artificial intelligence can automatically send follow-up emails to prospective parents following tours or enquiries.

Sample Tool:

Automated Follow-Ups: HubSpot AI

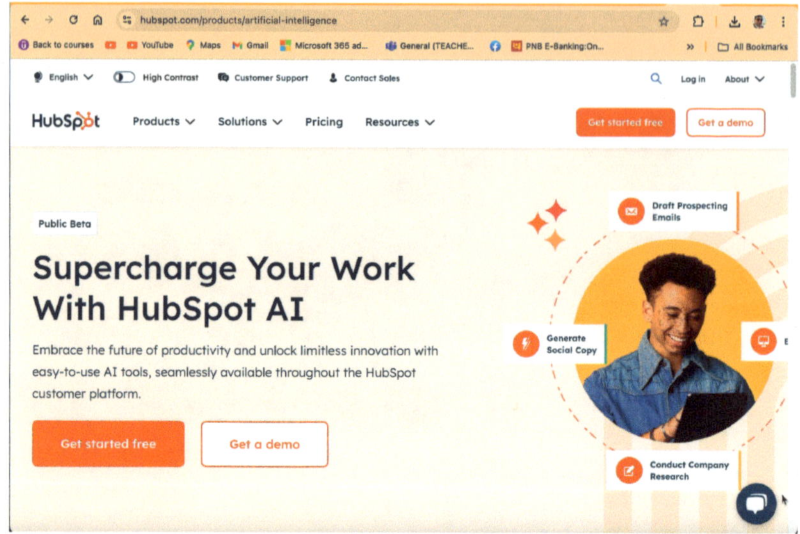

www.hubspot.com

16. Digital Assistants: Use AI-powered digital assistants to aid with academic enquiries and processes.

Sample Tool:

Digital Assistants: IBM Watson Assistant

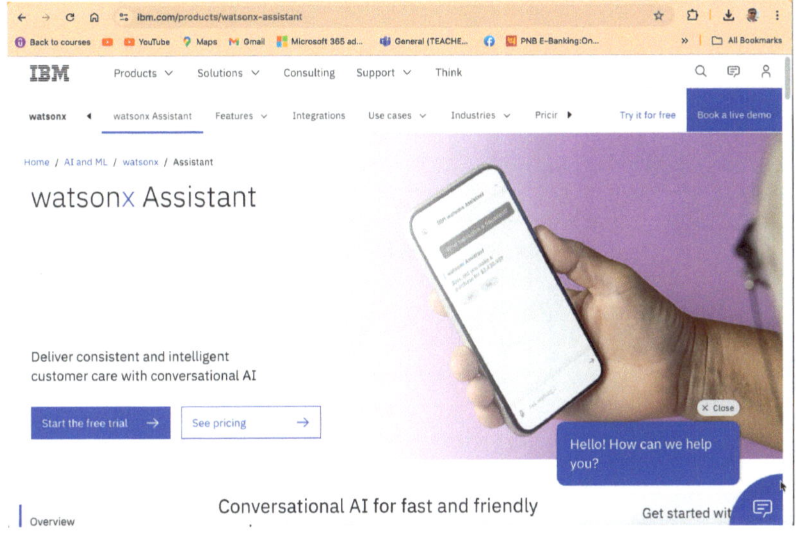
watsonx Assistant
Deliver consistent and intelligent customer care with conversational AI
Start the free trial
See pricing
Hello! How can we help you?
Conversational AI for fast and friendly
Overview

www.ibm.com/products/watsonx-assistant

17. Information Recommendations: AI can suggest appropriate information to parents and students based on their interactions.

Sample Tool:

Content Recommendations: Recombee

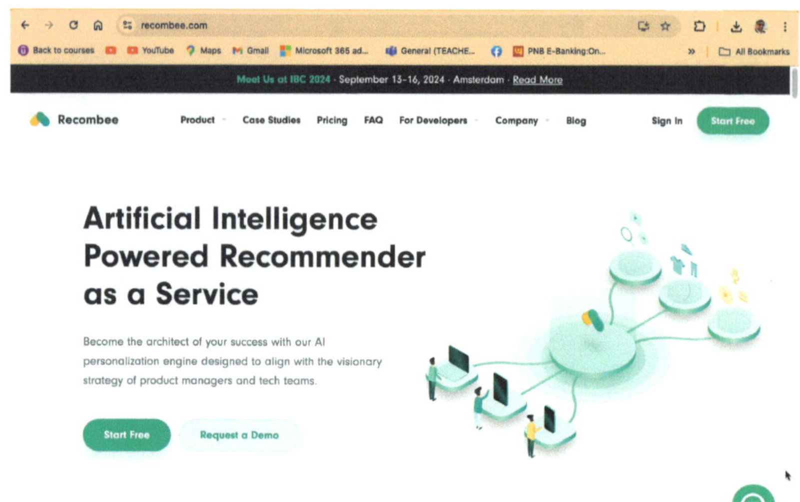

www.recombee.com

18. Sentiment Analysis: Use artificial intelligence to monitor internet sentiment about the institution and adapt marketing methods accordingly.

Sample Tool:

Sentiment Analysis: Brandwatch

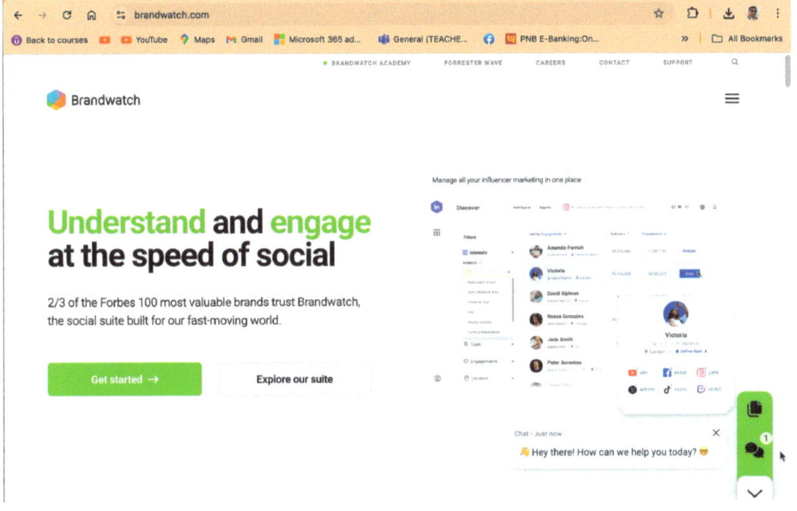

www.brandwatch.com

19. AI-Powered Enrolment Forms: Make the enrolment process easier with AI-powered forms that assist users seamlessly.

Sample Tool:

AI-Powered Enrollment Forms: JotForm AI

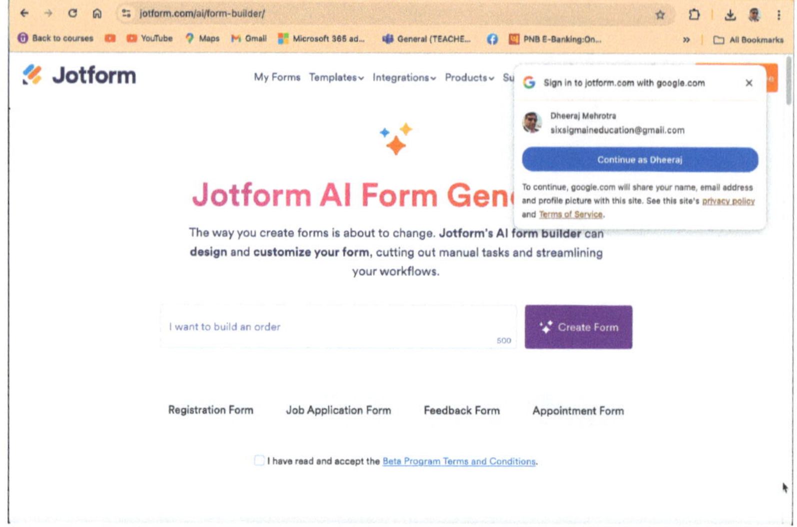
jotform.com/ai/form-builder/
Back to courses   YouTube   Maps   Gmail   Microsoft 365 ad...   General (TEACHE...   PNB E-Banking:On...   All Bookmarks
Jotform
My Forms   Templates   Integrations   Products   Su
Sign in to jotform.com with google.com
Dheeraj Mehrotra
sixsigmaineducation@gmail.com
Continue as Dheeraj
To continue, google.com will share your name, email address and profile picture with this site. See this site's privacy policy and Terms of Service.
Jotform AI Form Gen
The way you create forms is about to change. Jotform's AI form builder can design and customize your form, cutting out manual tasks and streamlining your workflows.
I want to build an order
500
Create Form
Registration Form   Job Application Form   Feedback Form   Appointment Form
I have read and accept the Beta Program Terms and Conditions.

www.jotform.com/ai/form-builder

20. Social Listening Tools: Use AI to listen to social media conversations and interact with parents about schooling.

Sample Tool:

Social Listening Tools: Talkwalker

21. Behavioural Targeting: AI can target parents depending on their internet activity and preferences.

Sample Tool:

Behavioural Targeting: Persado

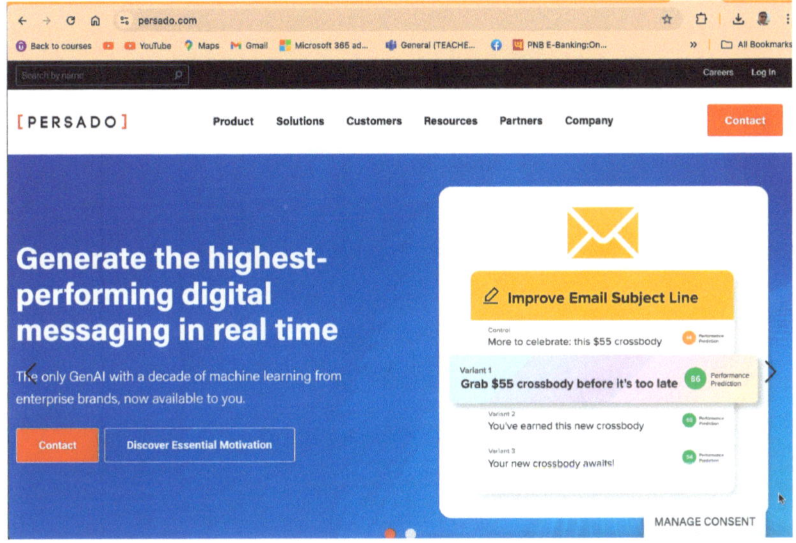

www.persado.com

22. Event Promotion: Artificial intelligence can help promote school activities by identifying and targeting interested parents and pupils.

Sample Tool:

Event Promotion: Eventbrite with AI integration

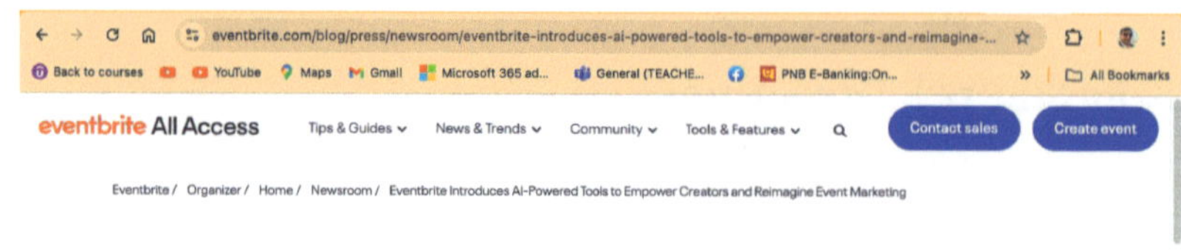

Eventbrite Introduces AI-Powered Tools to Empower Creators and Reimagine Event Marketing
eventbrite
Wildfire Music Fest
Write my ad

www.eventbrite.com

23. AI for Competitive Analysis: Use AI to analyse competitor strategies and improve the school's marketing strategy.

Sample Tool:

AI for Competitive Analysis: Crayon

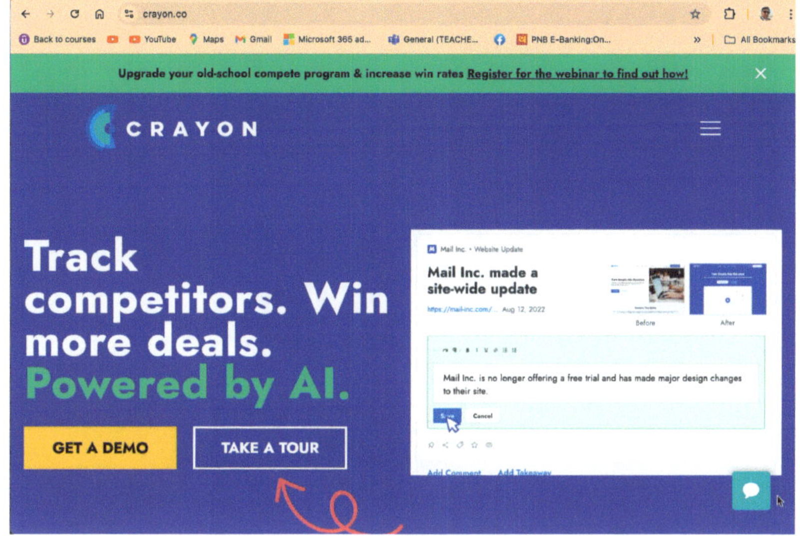

crayon.co
Back to courses   YouTube   Maps   Gmail   Microsoft 365 ad...   General (TEACHE...   PNB E-Banking:On...   All Bookmarks
Upgrade your old-school compete program & increase win rates Register for the webinar to find out how!
CRAYON
Track competitors. Win more deals. Powered by AI.
GET A DEMO
TAKE A TOUR
Mail Inc. • Website Update
Mail Inc. made a site-wide update
https://mail-inc.com/ ... Aug 12, 2022
Before
After
Mail Inc. is no longer offering a free trial and has made major design changes to their site.
Cancel
Add Comment   Add Takeaway

www.crayon.co

24. *Customised Brochures: Create AI-powered personalised brochures based on parental interests.*

Sample Tool:

Customized Brochures: Lucidpress AI

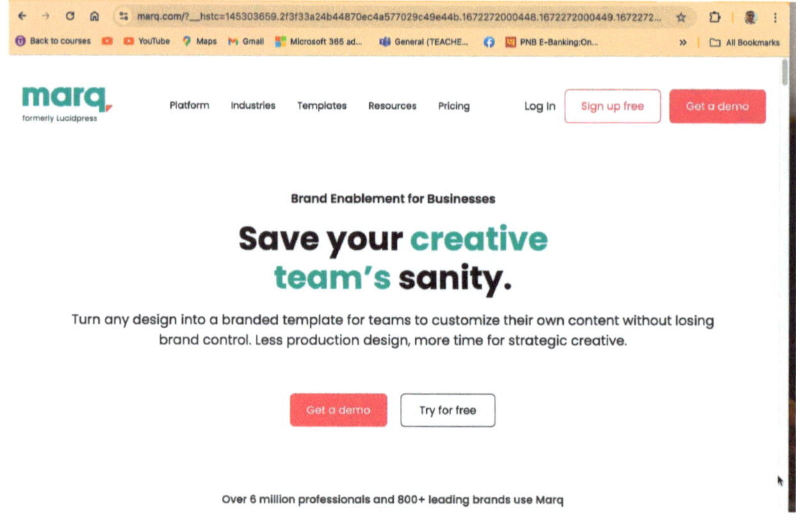
marq,
formerly Lucidpress
Platform   Industries   Templates   Resources   Pricing
Log In   Sign up free   Get a demo
Brand Enablement for Businesses
Save your creative team's sanity.
Turn any design into a branded template for teams to customize their own content without losing brand control. Less production design, more time for strategic creative.
Get a demo   Try for free
Over 6 million professionals and 800+ leading brands use Marq

www.marq.com

25. AI-Enhanced Blogging: AI can recommend blog subjects more likely to attract readers.

Sample Tool:

AI-Enhanced Blogging: MarketMuse

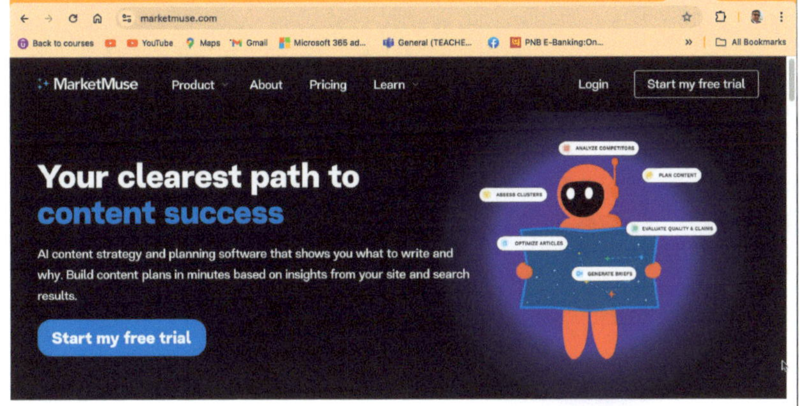

www.marketmuse.com

26. Lead Scoring: Artificial intelligence can rate leads based on their level of interaction, allowing you to prioritise follow-ups more effectively.

Sample Tool:

Lead Scoring: Salesforce Einstein

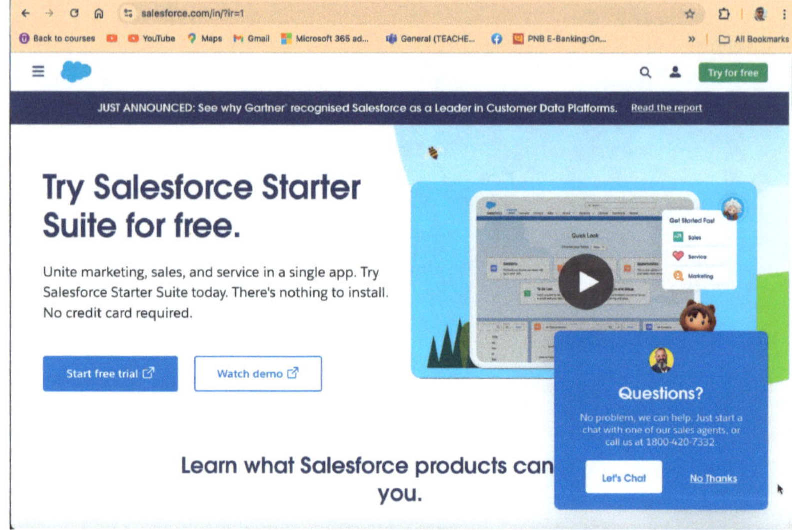
salesforce.com/in/?ir=1
JUST ANNOUNCED: See why Gartner recognised Salesforce as a Leader in Customer Data Platforms.   Read the report
Try for free
Try Salesforce Starter Suite for free.
Unite marketing, sales, and service in a single app. Try Salesforce Starter Suite today. There's nothing to install. No credit card required.
Start free trial
Watch demo
Learn what Salesforce products can you.
Questions?
No problem, we can help. Just start a chat with one of our sales agents, or call us at 1800-420-7332.
Let's Chat
No Thanks

www.salesforce.com

27. Automated Content Scheduling: *Artificial intelligence can automate the scheduling of social media postings to increase interaction.*

Sample Tool:

Automated Content Scheduling: Buffer with AI

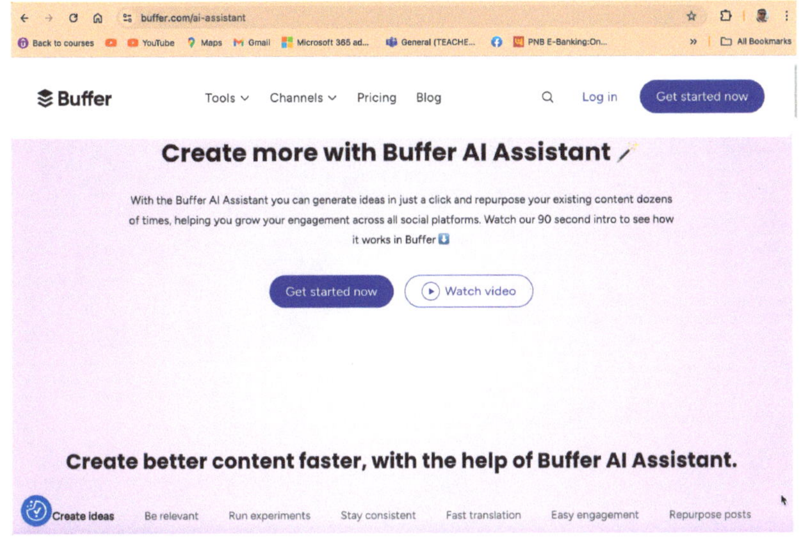
Buffer
Tools ⌄   Channels ⌄   Pricing   Blog
Log in
Get started now

Create more with Buffer AI Assistant

With the Buffer AI Assistant you can generate ideas in just a click and repurpose your existing content dozens of times, helping you grow your engagement across all social platforms. Watch our 90 second intro to see how it works in Buffer

Get started now
Watch video

Create better content faster, with the help of Buffer AI Assistant.

Create ideas   Be relevant   Run experiments   Stay consistent   Fast translation   Easy engagement   Repurpose posts

www.buffer.com/ai-assistant

28. Smart Email Campaigns: Artificial intelligence can segment email lists and send tailored campaigns to specific parent groups.

Sample Tool:

Smart Email Campaigns: Seventh Sense

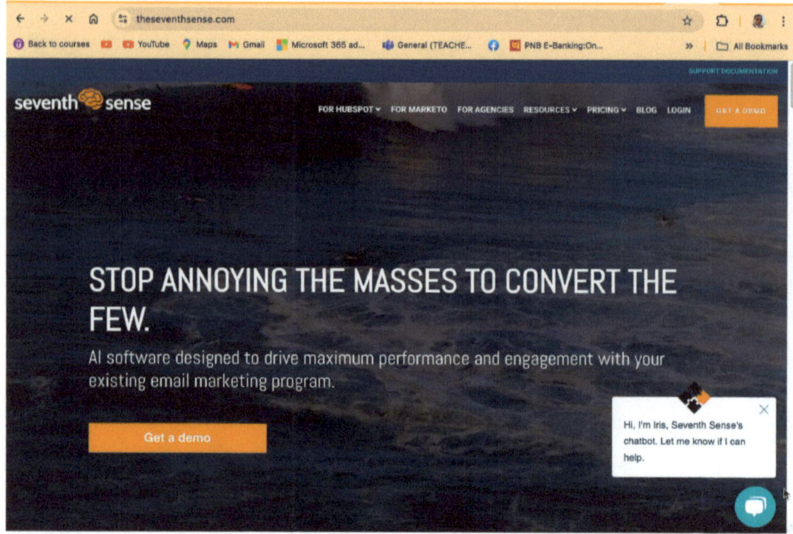
theseventhsense.com
Back to courses   YouTube   Maps   Gmail   Microsoft 365 ad...   General (TEACHE...   PNB E-Banking:On...   All Bookmarks
SUPPORT DOCUMENTATION
seventh sense
FOR HUBSPOT   FOR MARKETO   FOR AGENCIES   RESOURCES   PRICING   BLOG   LOGIN   GET A DEMO
STOP ANNOYING THE MASSES TO CONVERT THE FEW.
AI software designed to drive maximum performance and engagement with your existing email marketing program.
Get a demo
Hi, I'm Iris, Seventh Sense's chatbot. Let me know if I can help.

www.theseventhsense.com

29. AI-Optimized Ad Bidding: Use AI to improve ad bidding performance on platforms like Google Ads.

Sample Tool:

AI-Optimized Ad Bidding: Acquisio

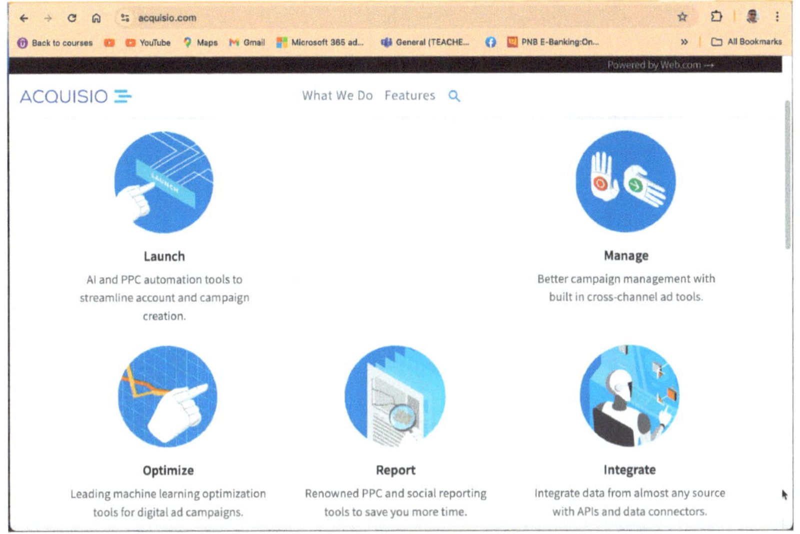

acquisio.com
Back to courses   YouTube   Maps   Gmail   Microsoft 365 ad...   General (TEACHE...   PNB E-Banking:On...   All Bookmarks
Powered by Web.com →
ACQUISIO
What We Do   Features
Launch
AI and PPC automation tools to streamline account and campaign creation.
Manage
Better campaign management with built in cross-channel ad tools.
Optimize
Leading machine learning optimization tools for digital ad campaigns.
Report
Renowned PPC and social reporting tools to save you more time.
Integrate
Integrate data from almost any source with APIs and data connectors.

www.acquisio.com

30. Automated Open House Invitations: AI may send personalised invitations to open houses and school functions.

Sample Tool:

Automated Open House Invitations: Constant Contact AI

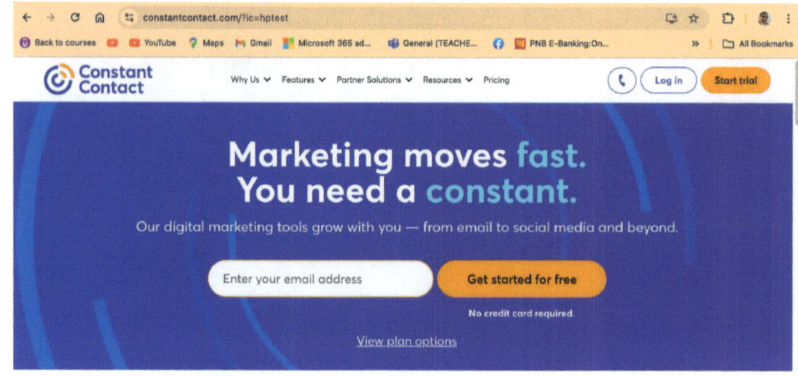
constantcontact.com/?ic=hptest
Back to courses   YouTube   Maps   Gmail   Microsoft 365 ad...   General (TEACHE...   PNB E-Banking:On...   All Bookmarks
Constant Contact
Why Us   Features   Partner Solutions   Resources   Pricing
Log in   Start trial
Marketing moves fast.
You need a constant.
Our digital marketing tools grow with you — from email to social media and beyond.
Enter your email address
Get started for free
No credit card required.
View plan options
How experienced are you with digital marketing?

www.constantcontact.com

31. AI-Powered Newsletters: Use AI to create dynamic newsletters based on the interests of each recipient.

Sample Tool:

AI-Powered Newsletters: rasa.io

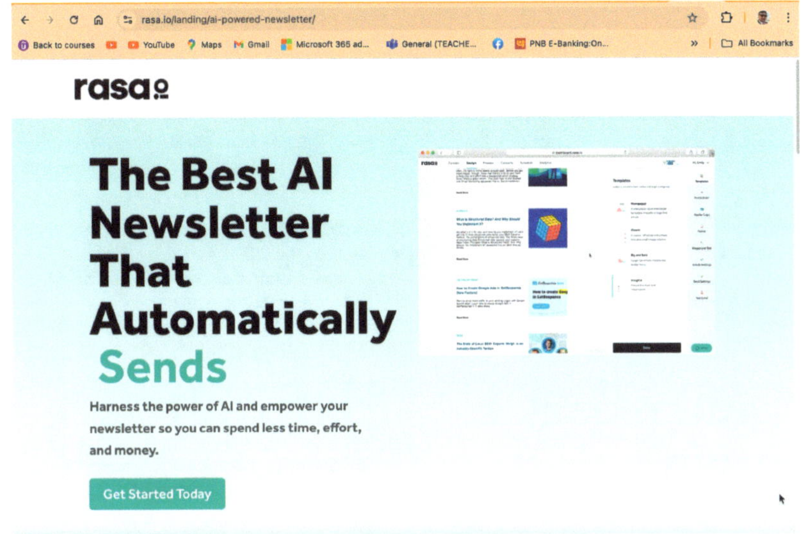
rasa.io
The Best AI
Newsletter
That
Automatically
Sends
Harness the power of AI and empower your
newsletter so you can spend less time, effort,
and money.
Get Started Today

www.rasa.io

32. Interactive Learning Demos: Provide AI-powered demonstrations of the school's educational resources and approaches.

Sample Tool:

Interactive Learning Demos: Articulate 360

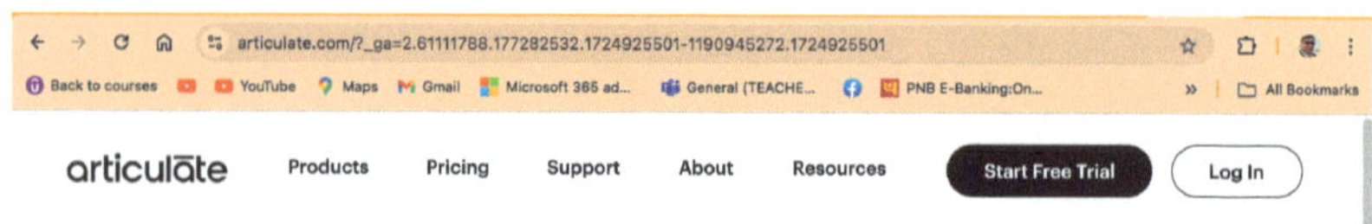

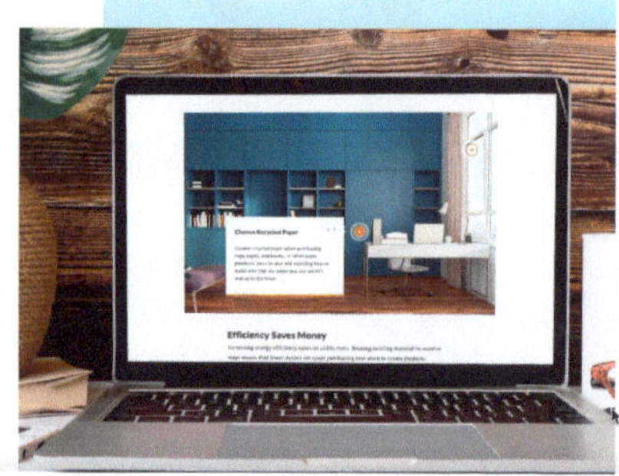
The #1
e-learning
platform for
creating
workplace
training
All the training tools you need to simplify

www.articulate.com

33. AI-Powered Parent Engagement: Utilise AI to identify and engage less involved parents through personalised outreach.

Sample Tool:

AI-Powered Parent Engagement: ParentSquare AI

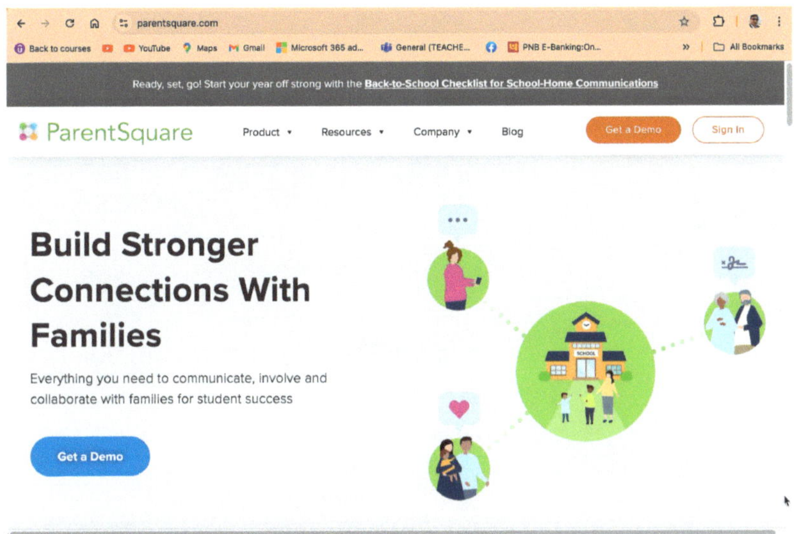
parentsquare.com
Back to courses
YouTube
Maps
Gmail
Microsoft 365 ad...
General (TEACHE...
PNB E-Banking:On...
All Bookmarks
Ready, set, go! Start your year off strong with the Back-to-School Checklist for School-Home Communications
ParentSquare
Product
Resources
Company
Blog
Get a Demo
Sign In
Build Stronger Connections With Families
Everything you need to communicate, involve and collaborate with families for student success
Get a Demo
SCHOOL

www.parentsquare.com

34. *Speech Recognition techniques*: Use AI to transcribe and distribute crucial school speeches or notifications.

Sample Tool:

Speech Recognition Techniques: Otter.ai

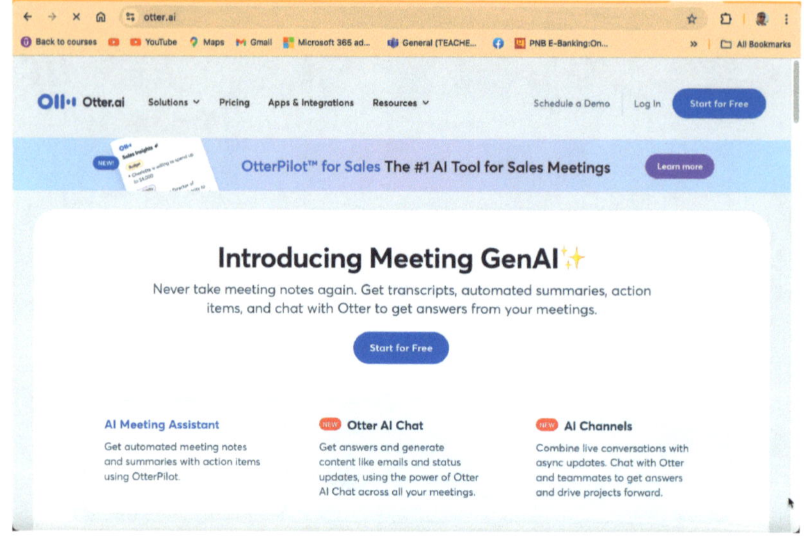
otter.ai
Back to courses   YouTube   Maps   Gmail   Microsoft 365 ad...   General (TEACHE...   PNB E-Banking:On...   All Bookmarks
Oll·I Otter.ai   Solutions ∨   Pricing   Apps & Integrations   Resources ∨   Schedule a Demo   Log In   Start for Free
NEW!   OtterPilot™ for Sales The #1 AI Tool for Sales Meetings   Learn more
Introducing Meeting GenAI
Never take meeting notes again. Get transcripts, automated summaries, action items, and chat with Otter to get answers from your meetings.
Start for Free
AI Meeting Assistant
Get automated meeting notes and summaries with action items using OtterPilot.
NEW   Otter AI Chat
Get answers and generate content like emails and status updates, using the power of Otter AI Chat across all your meetings.
NEW   AI Channels
Combine live conversations with async updates. Chat with Otter and teammates to get answers and drive projects forward.

www.otter.ai

35. AI-Generated Testimonials: Use AI to create testimonials based on favourable feedback and publish them on social media.

Sample Tool:

AI-Generated Testimonials: Testimonial.ai

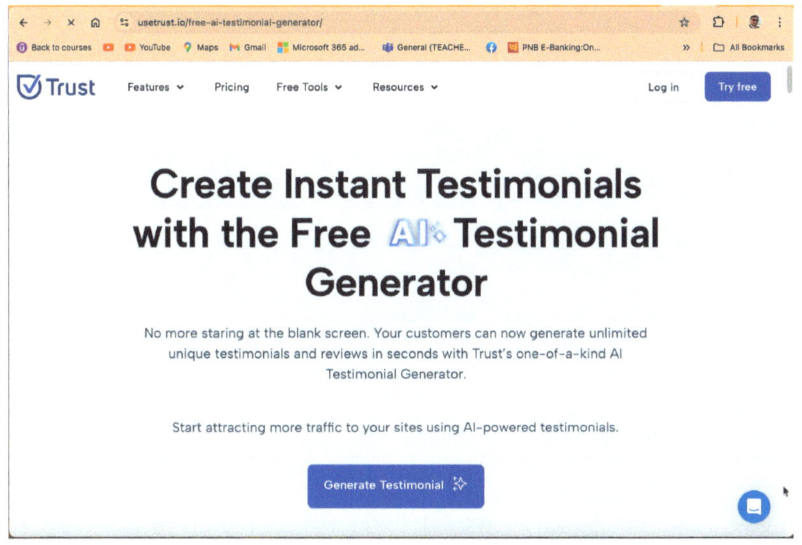
usetrust.io/free-ai-testimonial-generator/
Back to courses   YouTube   Maps   Gmail   Microsoft 365 ad...   General (TEACHE...   PNB E-Banking:On...   All Bookmarks
Trust   Features   Pricing   Free Tools   Resources   Log in   Try free
Create Instant Testimonials
with the Free AI Testimonial
Generator
No more staring at the blank screen. Your customers can now generate unlimited
unique testimonials and reviews in seconds with Trust's one-of-a-kind AI
Testimonial Generator.
Start attracting more traffic to your sites using AI-powered testimonials.
Generate Testimonial

www.usetrust.io

36. Personalised Learning Path Promotions: Use AI-generated content to promote the school's specific learning routes.

Sample Tool:

Personalized Learning Path Promotions: BrightBytes

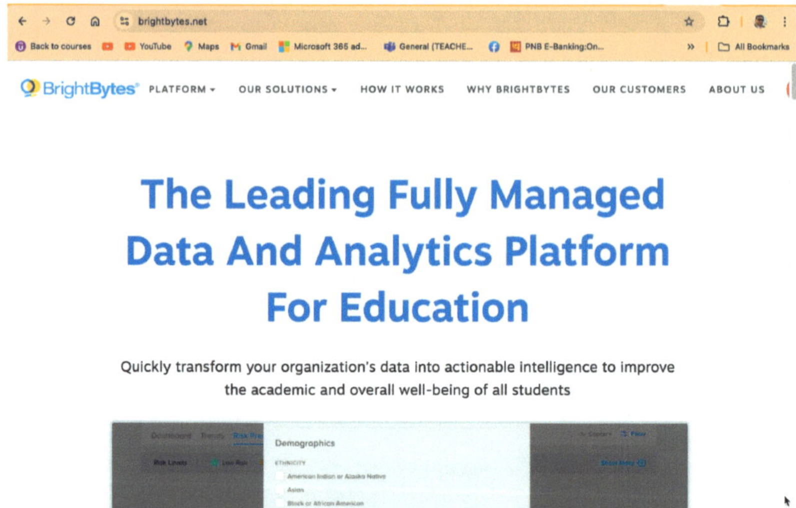

www.brightbytes.net

37. Automated Webinars: Use artificial intelligence to schedule and promote instructional webinars for parents.

Sample Tool:

Automated Webinars: EverWebinar

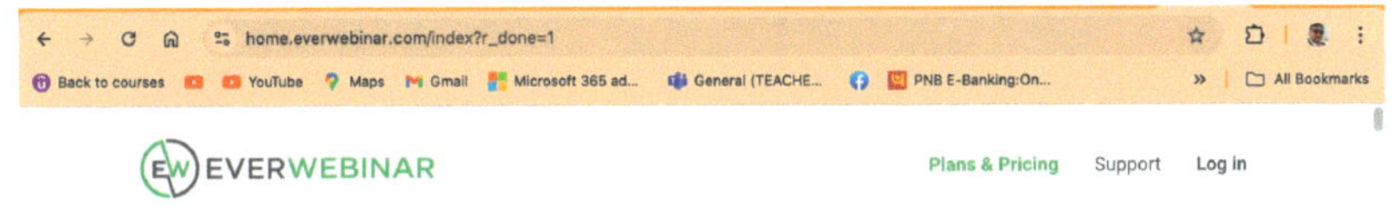

Deliver The Perfect Webinar
Presentation Over And Over Without
Ever Being Present
Automate your efforts and maximize your time with EverWebinar

www.home.everwebinar.com

38. AI in Parent Orientation: *Improve parent orientation programs by including AI-powered presentations and interactive sessions.*

Sample Tool:

AI in Parent Orientation: Prezi with AI

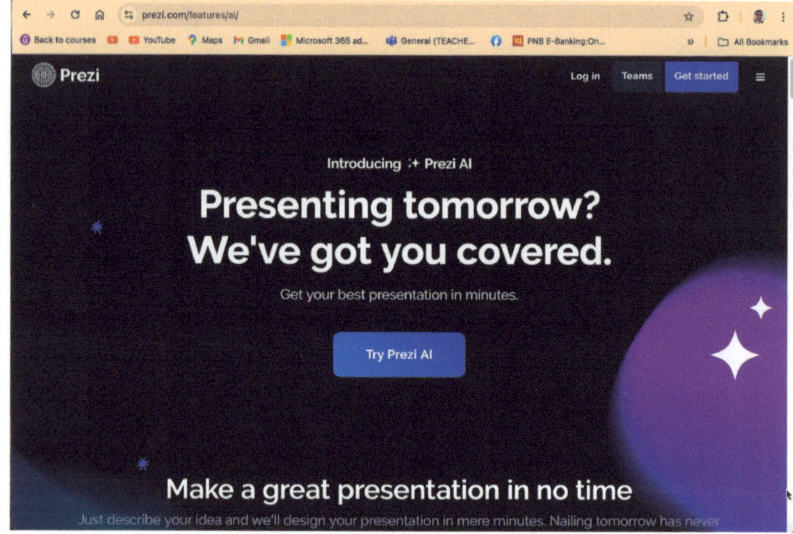
prezi.com/features/ai/
Back to courses   YouTube   Maps   Gmail   Microsoft 365 ad...   General (TEACHE...   PNB E-Banking:On...   All Bookmarks
Prezi
Log in   Teams   Get started
Introducing ✦ Prezi AI
Presenting tomorrow?
We've got you covered.
Get your best presentation in minutes.
Try Prezi AI
Make a great presentation in no time
Just describe your idea and we'll design your presentation in mere minutes. Nailing tomorrow has never

www.prezi.com

**39. Dynamic Ad material: AI may generate dynamic
ad material that responds to viewer engagement.**

Sample Tool:

Dynamic Ad Content: Adobe Sensei

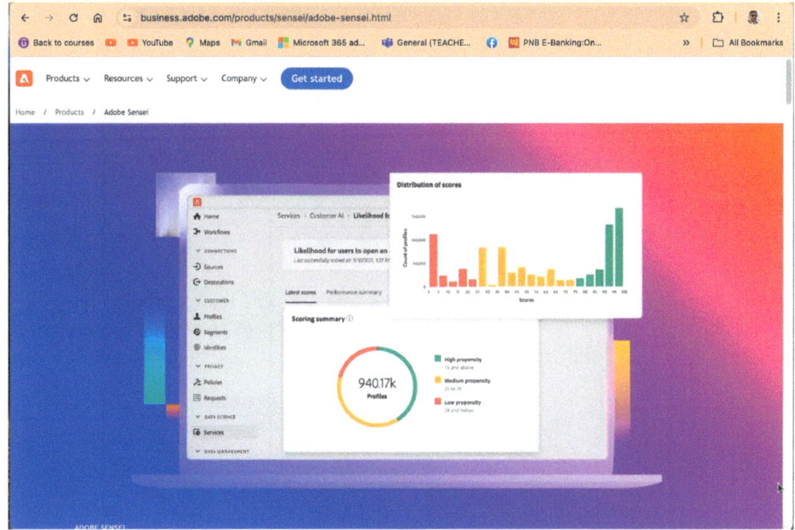

www.business.adobe.com

40. AI-Enhanced Webinars: Personalise and promote webinars for parents.

Sample Tool:

AI-Enhanced Webinars: Zoom AI Companion

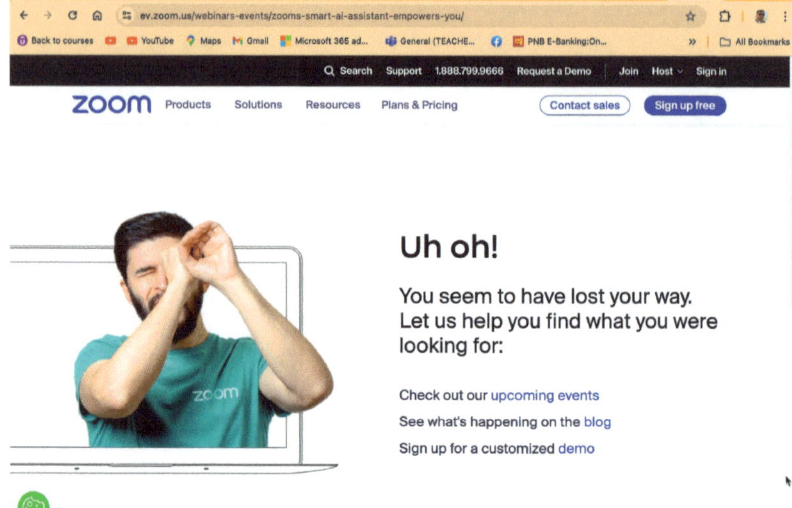
ev.zoom.us/webinars-events/zooms-smart-ai-assistant-empowers-you/
Back to courses   YouTube   Maps   Gmail   Microsoft 365 ad...   General (TEACHE...   PNB E-Banking:On...   All Bookmarks
Q Search   Support   1.888.799.9666   Request a Demo   Join   Host   Sign in
ZOOM   Products   Solutions   Resources   Plans & Pricing   Contact sales   Sign up free
Uh oh!
You seem to have lost your way.
Let us help you find what you were
looking for:
Check out our upcoming events
See what's happening on the blog
Sign up for a customized demo
zoom

www.ev.zoom.us

41. Online Reputation Management: Use AI to monitor and manage the school's online reputation.

Sample Tool:

Online Reputation Management: Yext

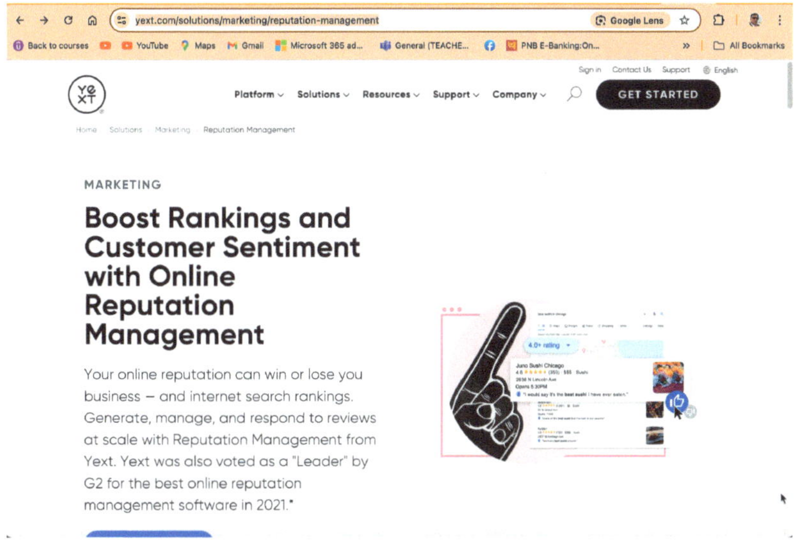

www.yext.com

42. Alumni Engagement: Artificial intelligence can identify and target alumni for school marketing activities.

Sample Tool:

Alumni Engagement: Graduway

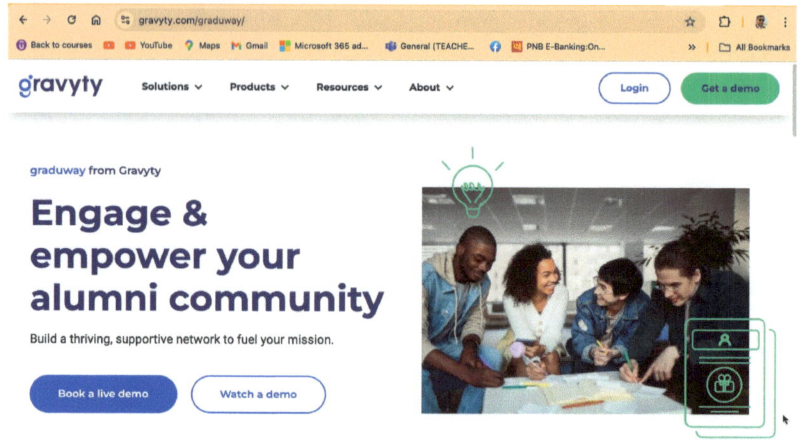
gravyty
Solutions ⌄   Products ⌄   Resources ⌄   About ⌄
Login
Get a demo
graduway from Gravyty
Engage & empower your alumni community
Build a thriving, supportive network to fuel your mission.
Book a live demo
Watch a demo

www.gravyty.com

43. Smart CRM Integration: Combine AI and CRM technology to personalise parent interactions.

Sample Tool:

Smart CRM Integration: Salesforce Einstein

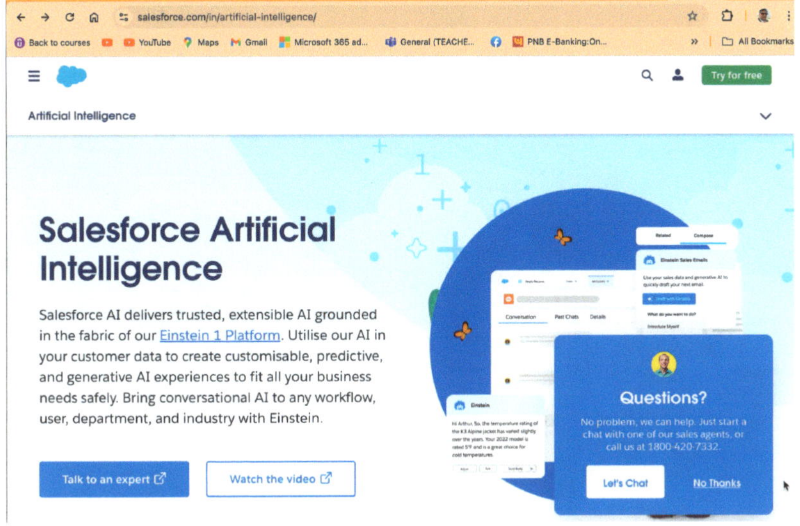
salesforce.com/in/artificial-intelligence/
Back to courses
YouTube
Maps
Gmail
Microsoft 365 ad...
General (TEACHE...
PNB E-Banking:On...
All Bookmarks
Try for free
Artificial Intelligence
Salesforce Artificial Intelligence
Salesforce AI delivers trusted, extensible AI grounded in the fabric of our Einstein 1 Platform. Utilise our AI in your customer data to create customisable, predictive, and generative AI experiences to fit all your business needs safely. Bring conversational AI to any workflow, user, department, and industry with Einstein.
Talk to an expert
Watch the video
Questions?
No problem, we can help. Just start a chat with one of our sales agents, or call us at 1800-420-7332.
Let's Chat
No Thanks

www.salesforce.com/in/artificial-intelligence/

44. Automated Event Registration: Artificial intelligence (AI) can streamline event registration processes, increasing customer experience.

Sample Tool:

Automated Event Registration: Cvent AI

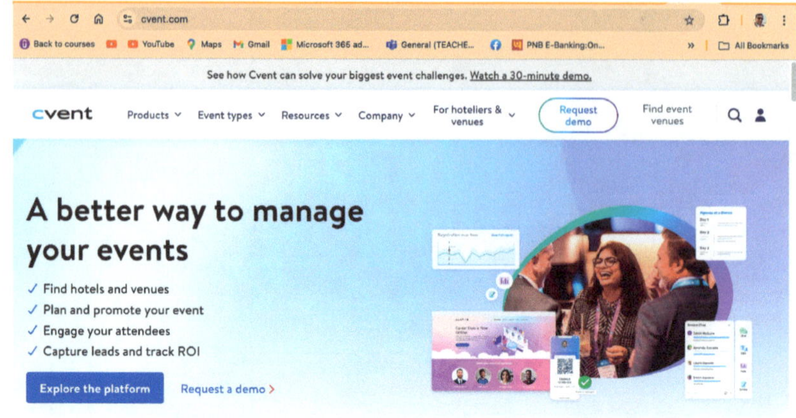

www.cvent.com

45. Content Translation: Use AI to translate marketing content into many languages for a varied audience.

Sample Tool:

Content Translation: DeepL

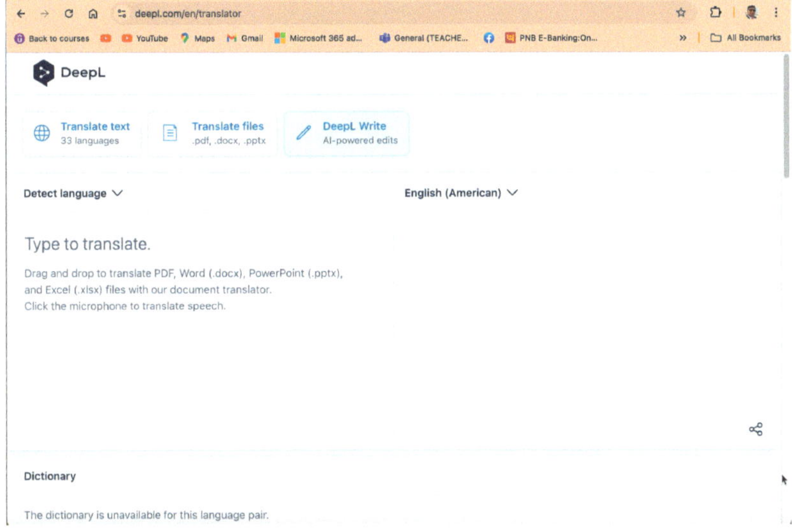

www.deepl.com/en/translator

46. Voice Search Optimisation: Prepare the school's website for AI-powered voice searches.

Sample Tool:

Voice Search Optimization: Alli AI

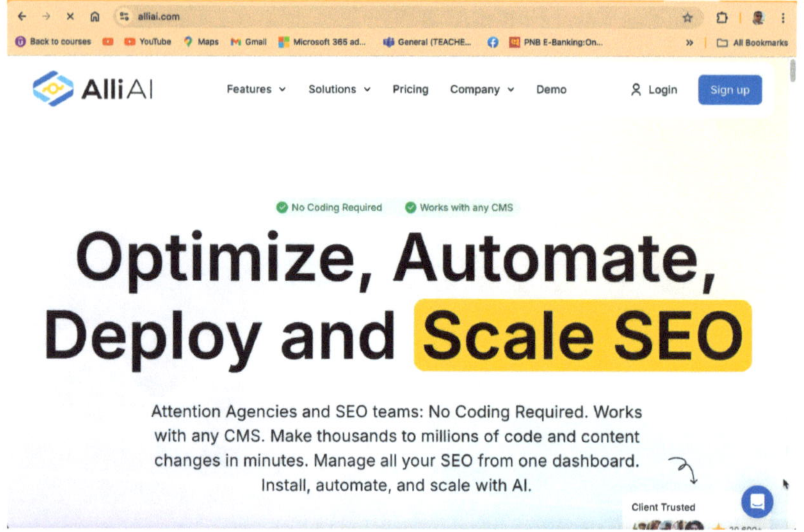
No Coding Required
Works with any CMS
Optimize, Automate, Deploy and Scale SEO
Attention Agencies and SEO teams: No Coding Required. Works with any CMS. Make thousands to millions of code and content changes in minutes. Manage all your SEO from one dashboard. Install, automate, and scale with AI.
Client Trusted
AlliAI
Features
Solutions
Pricing
Company
Demo
Login
Sign up

www.alliai.com

47. AI-Powered Infographics: Use AI to represent the school's successes and values visually.

Sample Tool:

AI-Powered Infographics: Venngage AI

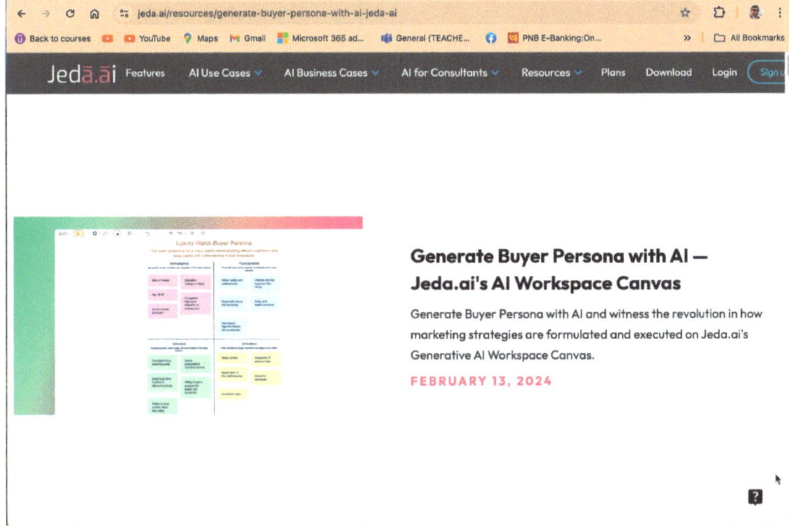

www.jeda.ai

48. Parent Persona Development: Artificial intelligence can assist in creating detailed parent personas for targeted marketing.

Sample Tool:

Generate Buyer Persona with AI — Jeda.ai's

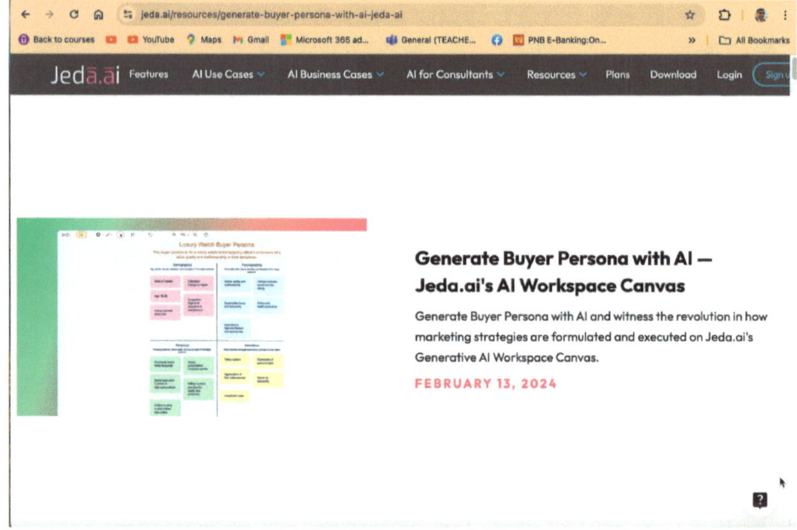

www.jeda.ai

49. Predictive information: Artificial intelligence can predict the type of information parents find most engaging and develop appropriately.

Sample Tool:

AI-Powered Recommender as a Service recombee

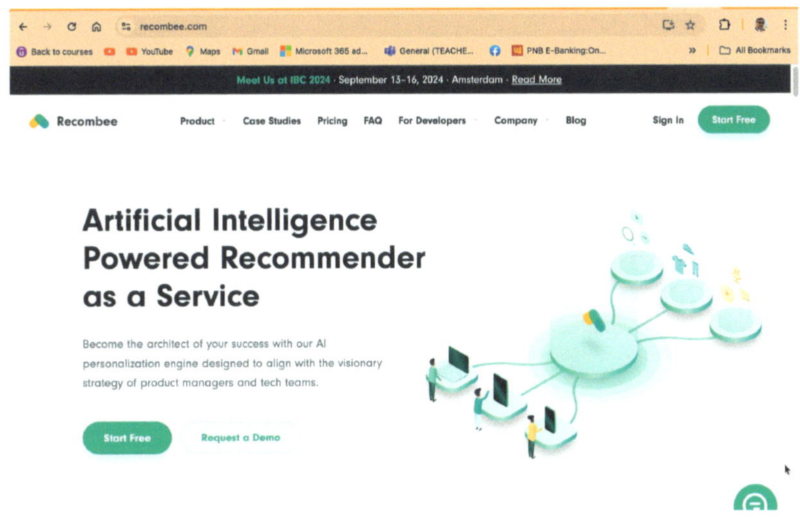
recombee.com
Back to courses   YouTube   Maps   Gmail   Microsoft 365 ad...   General (TEACHE...   PNB E-Banking:On...   All Bookmarks
Meet Us at IBC 2024 · September 13–16, 2024 · Amsterdam · Read More
Recombee   Product   Case Studies   Pricing   FAQ   For Developers   Company   Blog   Sign In   Start Free
Artificial Intelligence
Powered Recommender
as a Service
Become the architect of your success with our AI
personalization engine designed to align with the visionary
strategy of product managers and tech teams.
Start Free   Request a Demo

www.recombee.com

50. SEO Content Creation: Use AI tools to generate SEO-optimized content to boost the school's website traffic.

Sample Tool:

. SEO Content Creation: Clearscope

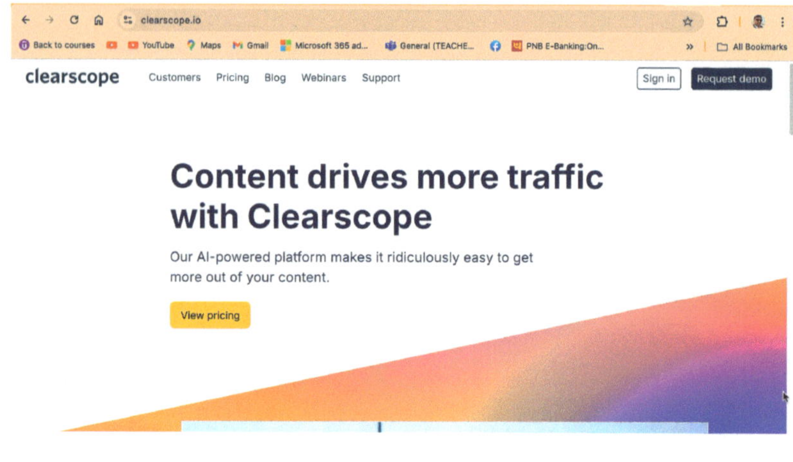

clearscope
Customers   Pricing   Blog   Webinars   Support
Sign in
Request demo
Content drives more traffic with Clearscope
Our AI-powered platform makes it ridiculously easy to get more out of your content.
View pricing

www.clearscope.io

51. Data-Driven Content Strategy: Create a content strategy using AI-powered data analysis on parent interests.

Sample Tool:

Data-Driven Content Strategy: Parse.ly

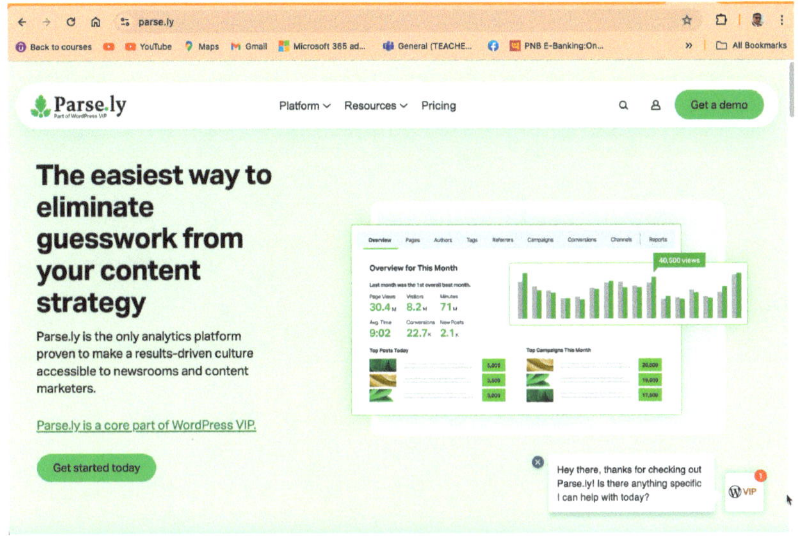
Parse.ly
Part of WordPress VIP
Platform
Resources
Pricing
Get a demo
The easiest way to eliminate guesswork from your content strategy
Parse.ly is the only analytics platform proven to make a results-driven culture accessible to newsrooms and content marketers.
Parse.ly is a core part of WordPress VIP.
Get started today
Overview for This Month
Last month was the 1st overall best month.
Page Views
30.4 M
Visitors
8.2 M
Minutes
71 M
Avg. Time
9:02
Conversions
22.7 K
New Posts
2.1 K
40,500 views
Top Posts Today
Top Campaigns This Month
Hey there, thanks for checking out Parse.ly! Is there anything specific I can help with today?

www.parse.ly

52. AI-Enhanced School Branding: Use AI to improve and market the school's brand image.

Sample Tool:

AI-Enhanced School Branding: Tailor Brands

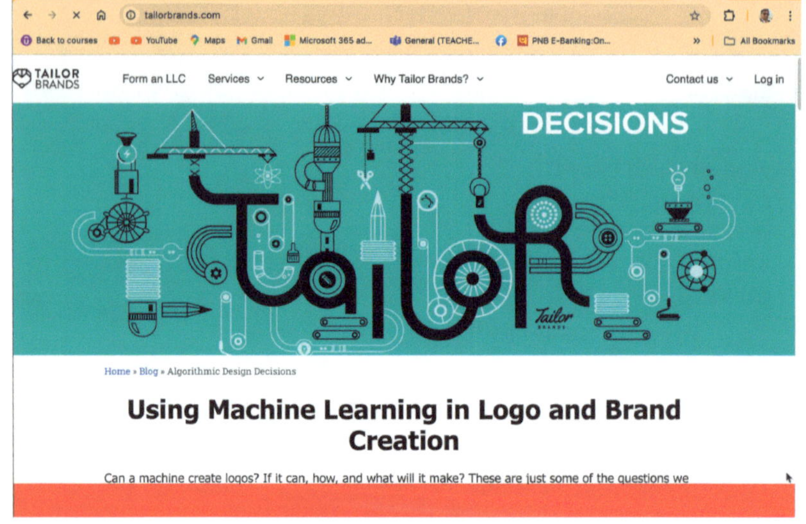

www.tailorbrands.com

53. AI for Scheduling Tours: Use AI to automate school tour scheduling, giving parents more flexibility and convenience.

Sample Tool:

AI for Scheduling Tours: Calendly with AI

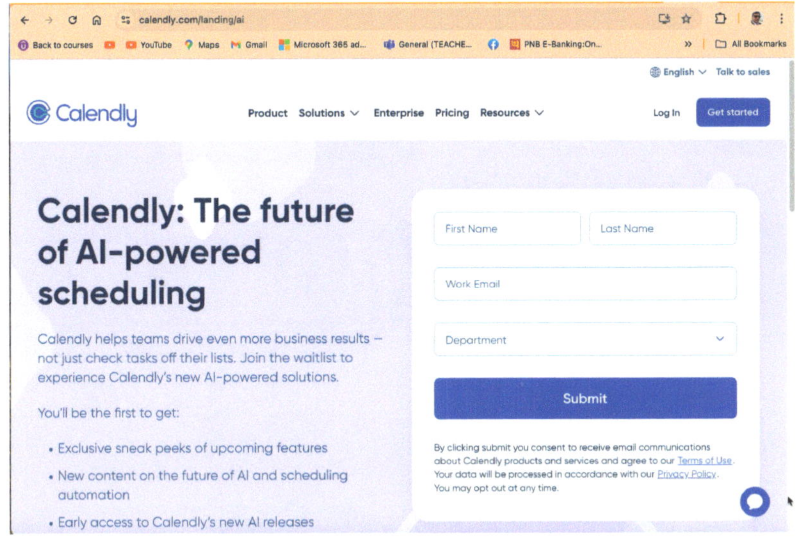
calendly.com/landing/ai
Back to courses   YouTube   Maps   Gmail   Microsoft 365 ad...   General (TEACHE...   PNB E-Banking:On...   »   All Bookmarks
English   Talk to sales
Calendly
Product   Solutions   Enterprise   Pricing   Resources
Log In   Get started
Calendly: The future of AI-powered scheduling
Calendly helps teams drive even more business results — not just check tasks off their lists. Join the waitlist to experience Calendly's new AI-powered solutions.
You'll be the first to get:
Exclusive sneak peeks of upcoming features
New content on the future of AI and scheduling automation
Early access to Calendly's new AI releases
First Name
Last Name
Work Email
Department
Submit
By clicking submit you consent to receive email communications about Calendly products and services and agree to our Terms of Use. Your data will be processed in accordance with our Privacy Policy. You may opt out at any time.

www.calendly.com/landing/ai

54. Interactive AI Campaigns: Design interactive campaigns that engage parents with quizzes and personalised material.

Sample Tool:

Interactive AI Campaigns: Outgrow

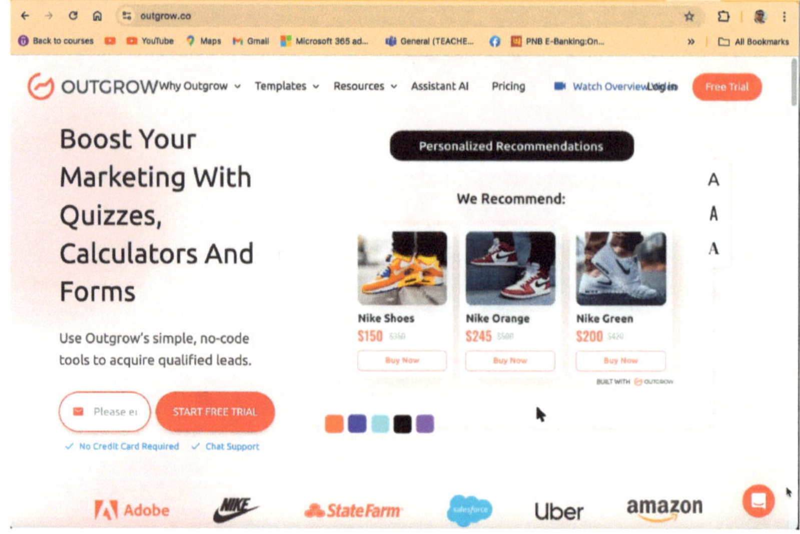

www.outgrow.co

55. AI-Powered Parental Insights: AI-driven data analysis can provide insight into parental requirements and concerns.

Sample Tool:

AI-Powered Parental Insights: Qlik Sense

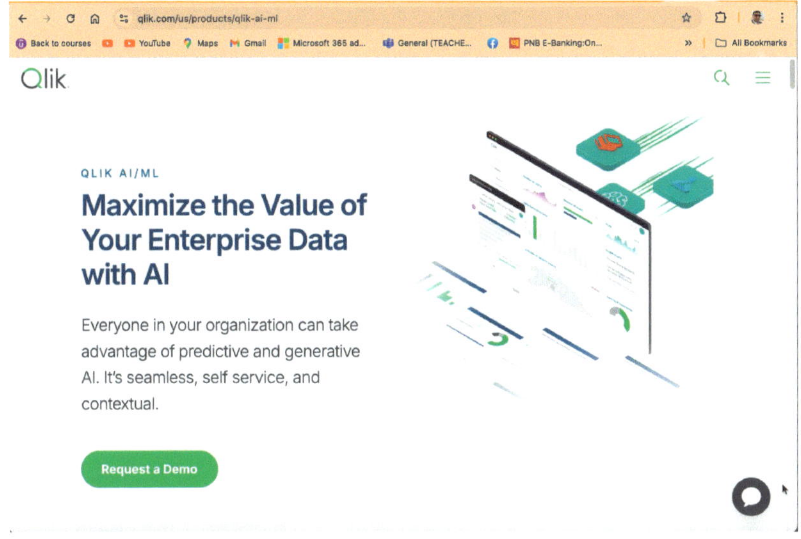

qlik.com/us/products/qlik-ai-ml
Back to courses   YouTube   Maps   Gmail   Microsoft 365 ad...   General (TEACHE...   PNB E-Banking:On...   All Bookmarks
Qlik
QLIK AI/ML
Maximize the Value of
Your Enterprise Data
with AI
Everyone in your organization can take
advantage of predictive and generative
AI. It's seamless, self service, and
contextual.
Request a Demo

www.qlik.com

56. Automated Parent Surveys: Use artificial intelligence to distribute and analyse parental satisfaction surveys.

Sample Tool:

Parent Surveys: SurveyMonkey AI

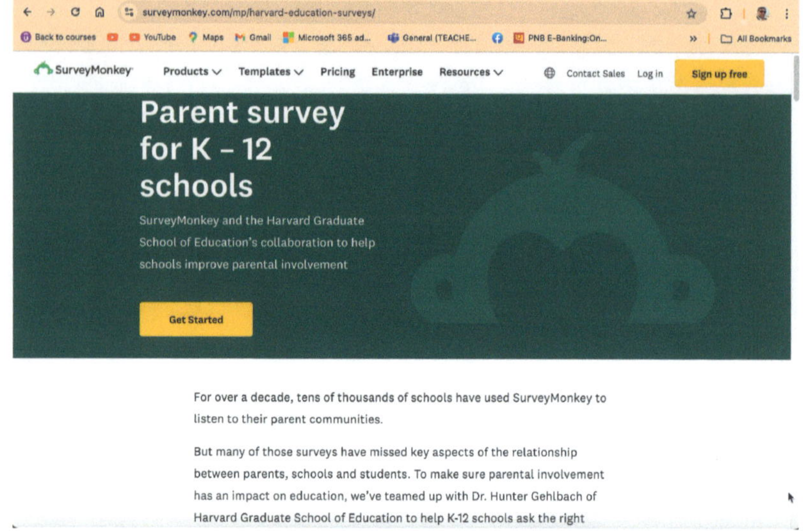

surveymonkey.com/mp/harvard-education-surveys/
Back to courses
YouTube
Maps
Gmail
Microsoft 365 ad...
General (TEACHE...
PNB E-Banking:On...
All Bookmarks
SurveyMonkey
Products
Templates
Pricing
Enterprise
Resources
Contact Sales
Log in
Sign up free
Parent survey
for K – 12
schools
SurveyMonkey and the Harvard Graduate
School of Education's collaboration to help
schools improve parental involvement
Get Started
For over a decade, tens of thousands of schools have used SurveyMonkey to
listen to their parent communities.
But many of those surveys have missed key aspects of the relationship
between parents, schools and students. To make sure parental involvement
has an impact on education, we've teamed up with Dr. Hunter Gehlbach of
Harvard Graduate School of Education to help K-12 schools ask the right

www.surveymonkey.com

57. Smart Brochure Distribution: Artificial intelligence can help disseminate digital brochures to specific consumers.

Sample Tool:

Smart Brochure Distribution: Foleon

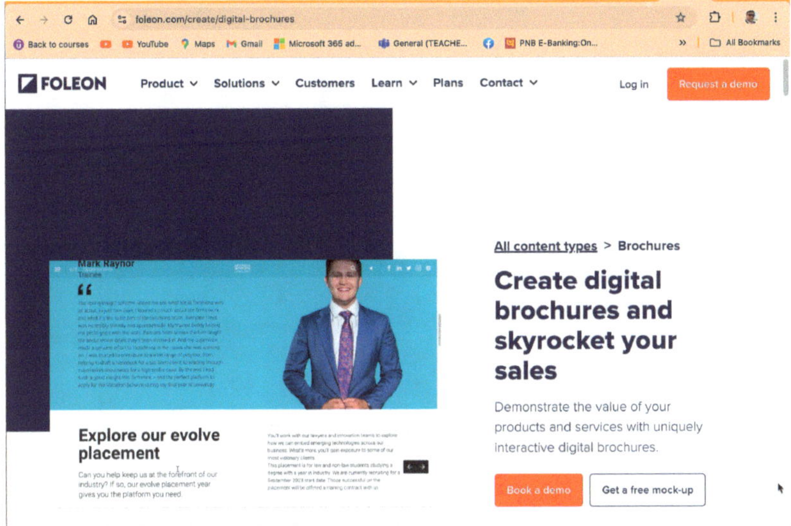

www.foleon.com

58. Social Media Influencer Targeting: Use AI to find and engage local influencers for school marketing.

Sample Tool:

Social Media Influencer Targeting: Upfluence

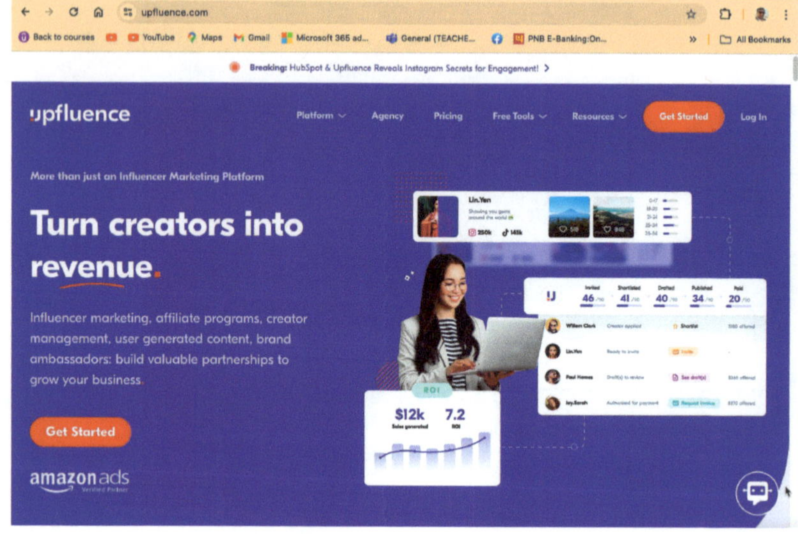
upfluence
Platform
Agency
Pricing
Free Tools
Resources
Get Started
Log In
More than just an Influencer Marketing Platform
Turn creators into revenue.
Influencer marketing, affiliate programs, creator management, user generated content, brand ambassadors: build valuable partnerships to grow your business.
Get Started
amazon ads
upfluence.com
Breaking: HubSpot & Upfluence Reveals Instagram Secrets for Engagement!
$12k
Sales generated
7.2
ROI

www.upfluence.com

59. Predictive Marketing Models: Use AI to anticipate the performance of different marketing campaigns.

Sample Tool:

Predictive Marketing Models: DataRobot

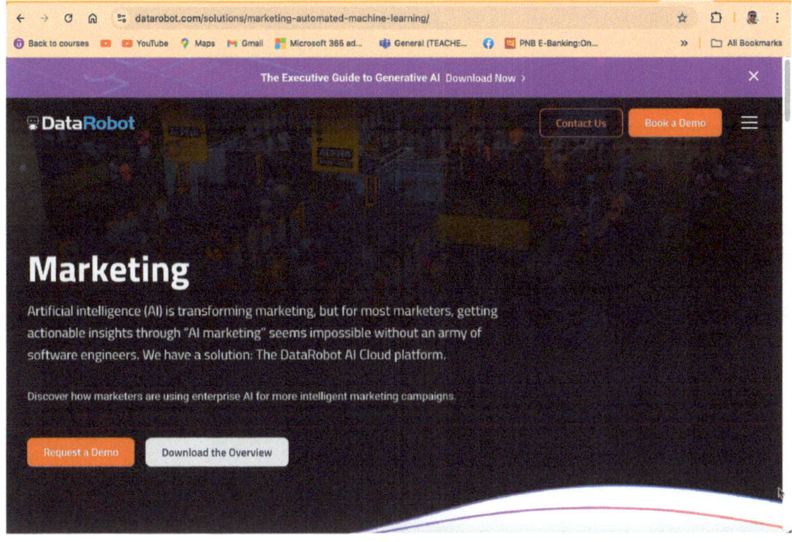

datarobot.com/solutions/marketing-automated-machine-learning/
The Executive Guide to Generative AI Download Now ›
DataRobot
Contact Us
Book a Demo
Marketing
Artificial intelligence (AI) is transforming marketing, but for most marketers, getting actionable insights through "AI marketing" seems impossible without an army of software engineers. We have a solution: The DataRobot AI Cloud platform.
Discover how marketers are using enterprise AI for more intelligent marketing campaigns.
Request a Demo
Download the Overview

www.datarobot.com

60. *Voice-Activated material*: Create AI-powered voice-activated material to keep parents engaged.

Sample Tool:

Voice-Activated Content: Voiceflow

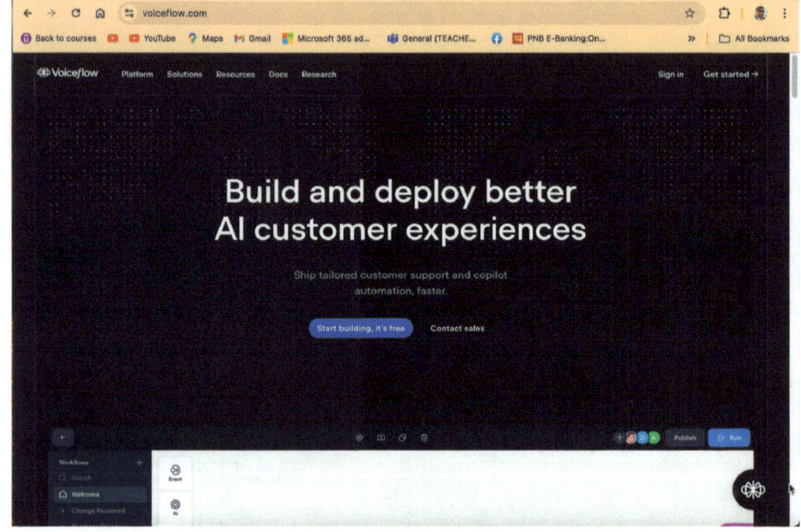

www.voiceflow.com

61. AI for Personalised Marketing: Create marketing campaigns based on unique parent preferences.

Sample Tool:

AI for Personalized Marketing: Dynamic Yield

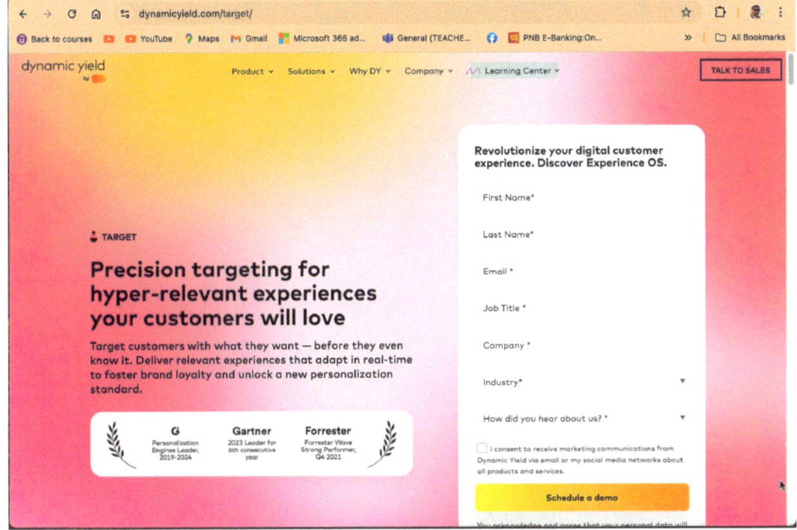

www.dynamicyield.com

62. Dynamic Landing Pages: AI may generate dynamic landing pages based on visitor behaviour and preferences.

Sample Tool:

Dynamic Landing Pages: Unbounce with AI

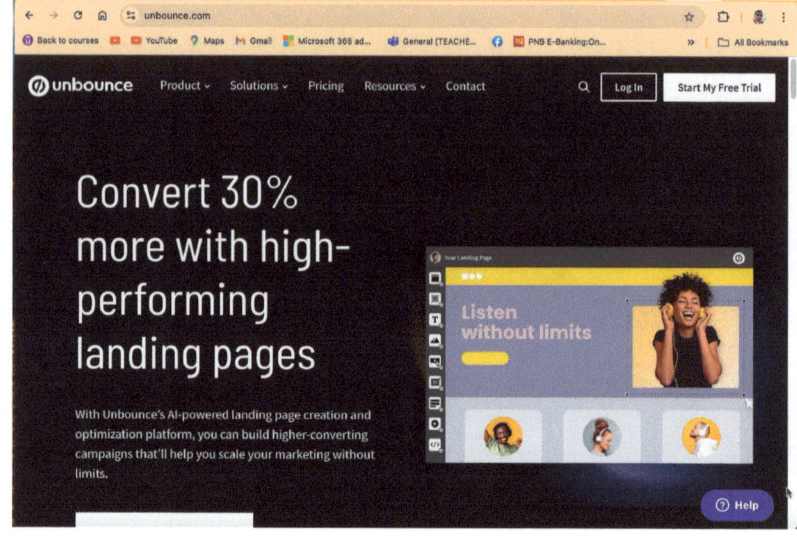
unbounce
Product
Solutions
Pricing
Resources
Contact
Log In
Start My Free Trial
Convert 30% more with high-performing landing pages
With Unbounce's AI-powered landing page creation and optimization platform, you can build higher-converting campaigns that'll help you scale your marketing without limits.
Listen without limits
Help

www.unbounce.com

63. AI-Enhanced Storytelling: Use AI to create engaging narratives highlighting the school's strengths.

Sample Tool:

AI-Enhanced Storytelling: Narrative Science

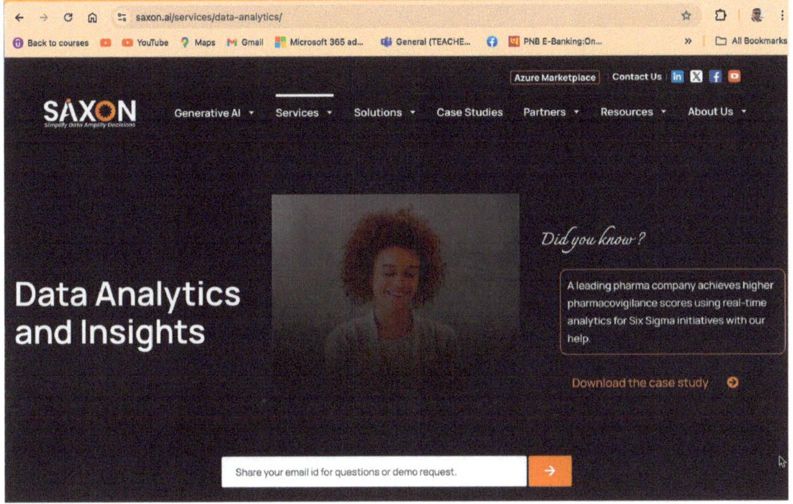
Azure Marketplace
Contact Us
SAXON
Simplify Data Amplify Decisions
Generative AI
Services
Solutions
Case Studies
Partners
Resources
About Us
Data Analytics
and Insights
Did you know ?
A leading pharma company achieves higher pharmacovigilance scores using real-time analytics for Six Sigma initiatives with our help.
Download the case study
Share your email id for questions or demo request.

www.saxon.ai

64. *Multichannel Marketing:* AI *can optimise marketing across many channels while maintaining a consistent message.*

Sample Tool:

Multichannel Marketing: Omnisend

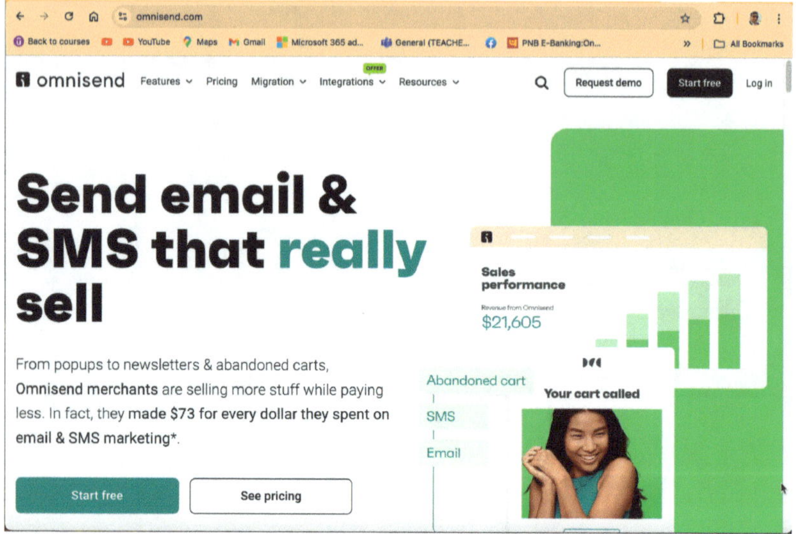
omnisend
Features
Pricing
Migration
Integrations
Resources
Request demo
Start free
Log in
Send email &
SMS that really
sell
From popups to newsletters & abandoned carts,
Omnisend merchants are selling more stuff while paying
less. In fact, they made $73 for every dollar they spent on
email & SMS marketing*.
Start free
See pricing
Sales performance
Revenue from Omnisend
$21,605
Abandoned cart
SMS
Email
Your cart called

www.omnisend.com

**65. Data-Driven Decision Making: Using AI, make
intelligent marketing decisions based on real-time
data.**

Sample Tool:

Data-Driven Decision Making: Looker

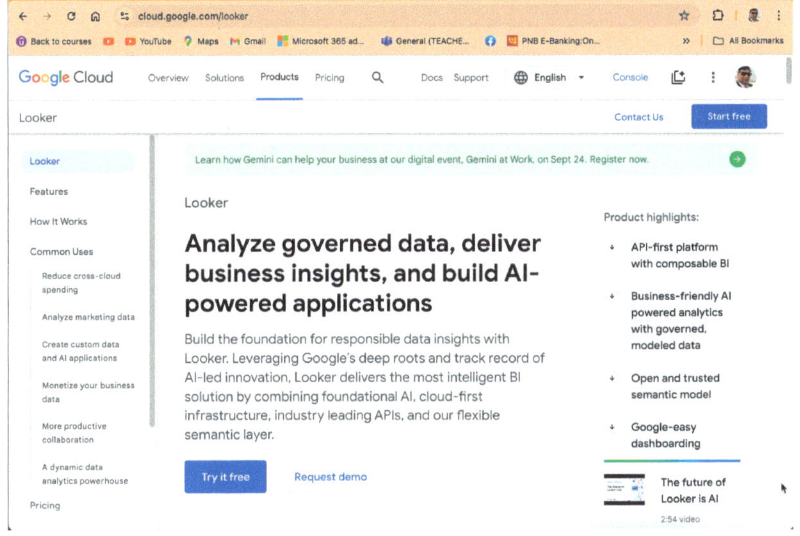

www.cloud.google.com

66. AI-Driven Ad Placement: AI can optimise where and when advertisements are displayed to successfully reach the intended audience.

Sample Tool:

AI-Driven Ad Placement: Albert.ai

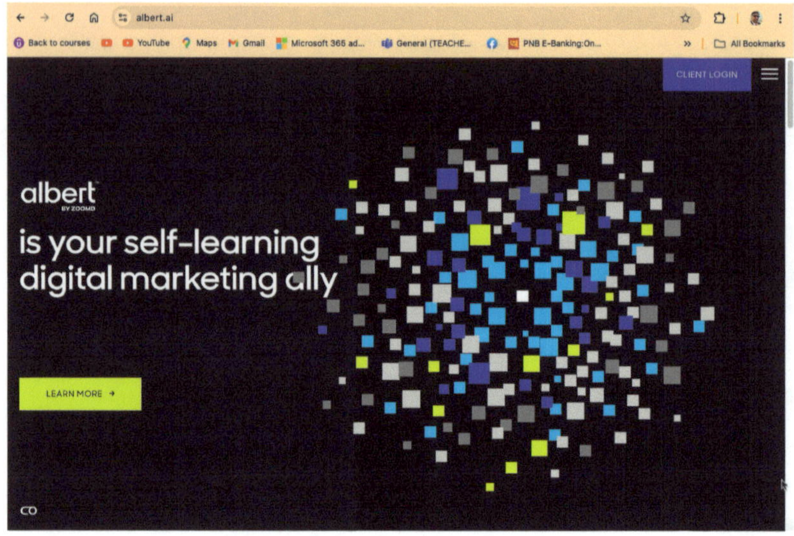

www.albert.ai

67. Automated Follow-Up Emails: *Artificial intelligence can generate automated follow-up emails responding to enquiries or events.*

Sample Tool:

Automated Follow-Up Emails: Drift

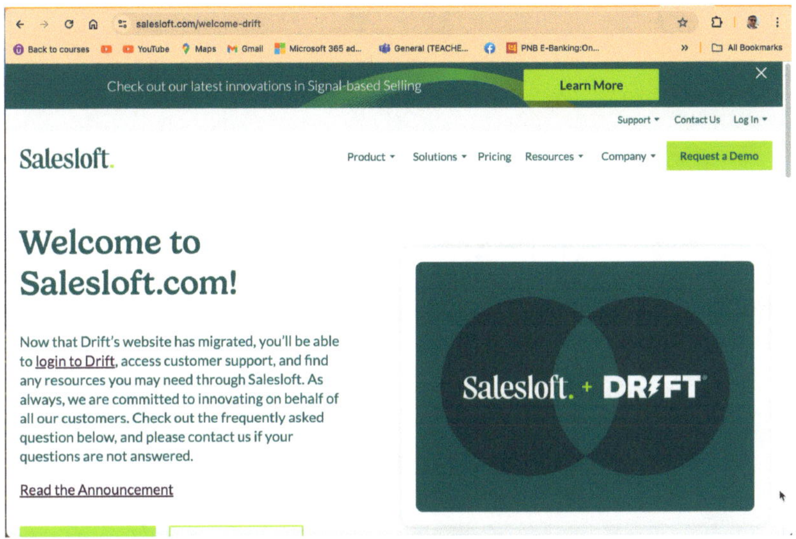
salesloft.com/welcome-drift
Back to courses   YouTube   Maps   Gmail   Microsoft 365 ad...   General (TEACHE...   PNB E-Banking:On...   All Bookmarks
Check out our latest innovations in Signal-based Selling   Learn More
Support   Contact Us   Log In
Salesloft.
Product   Solutions   Pricing   Resources   Company   Request a Demo
Welcome to
Salesloft.com!
Now that Drift's website has migrated, you'll be able
to login to Drift, access customer support, and find
any resources you may need through Salesloft. As
always, we are committed to innovating on behalf of
all our customers. Check out the frequently asked
question below, and please contact us if your
questions are not answered.
Read the Announcement
Salesloft. + DRIFT

www.salesloft.com

68. Interactive Parent Portals: AI can improve parent portals by making them more entertaining and informative.

Sample Tool:

Interactive Parent Portals: Finalsite

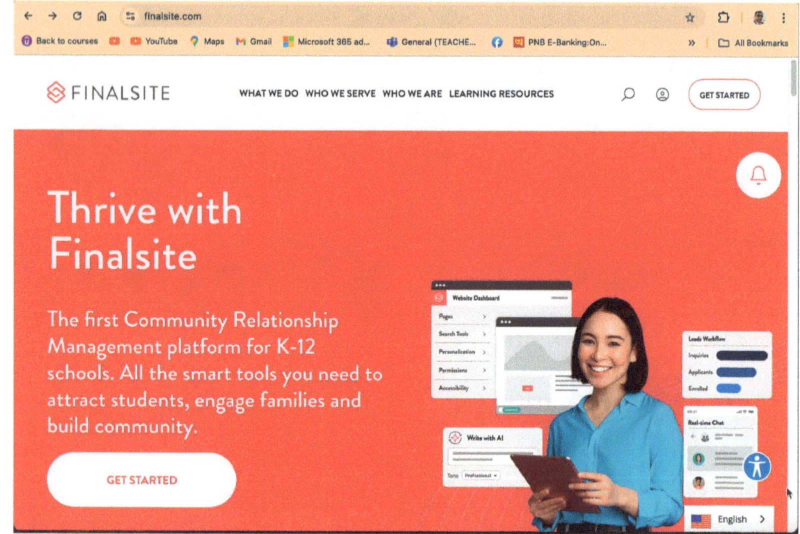

www.finalsite.com

69. AI-Powered Analytics Dashboards: Use AI to build dashboards that track and report on marketing performance.

Sample Tool:

AI-Powered Analytics Dashboards: Sisense

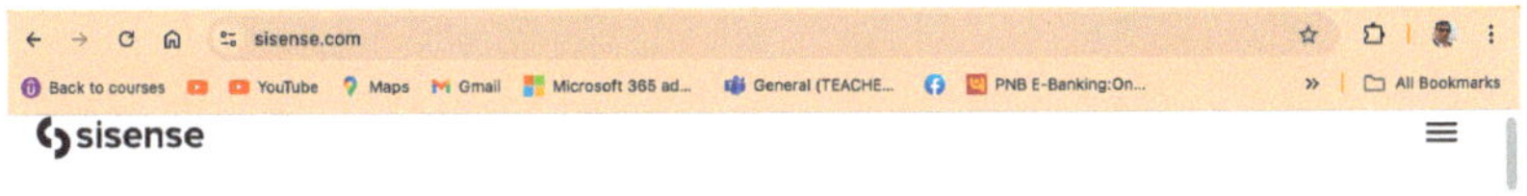

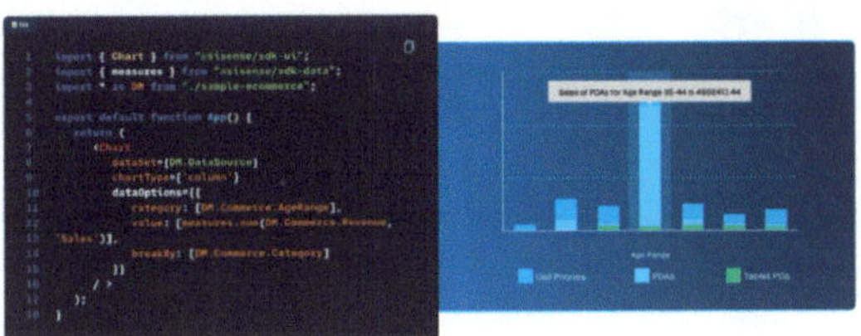

Fusion platform
Build analytics in your application

www.sisense.com

70. Personalised Video Messages: Make personalised video messages for parents with AI-powered video tools.

Sample Tool:

Personalized Video Messages: Vidyard

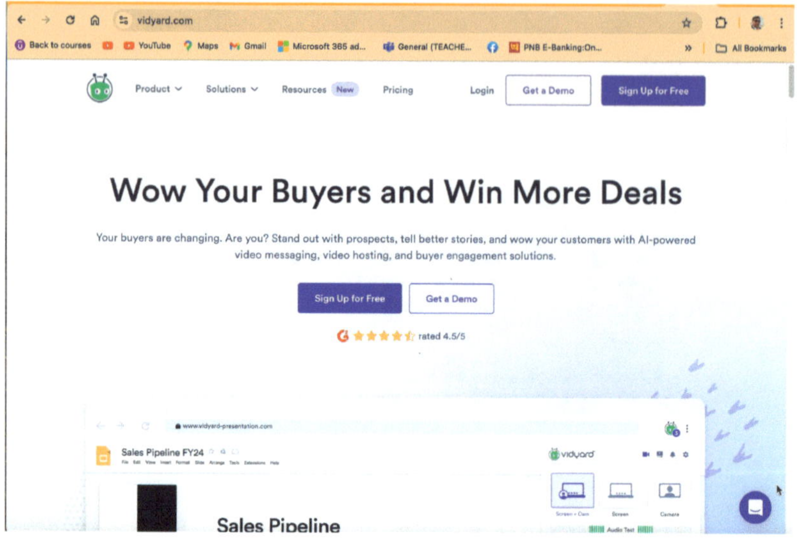

www.vidyard.com

**71. AI in School Open Days: Improve open days by
including AI-powered presentations and
personalised parent engagement.**

Sample Tool:

AI in School Open Days: Hopin

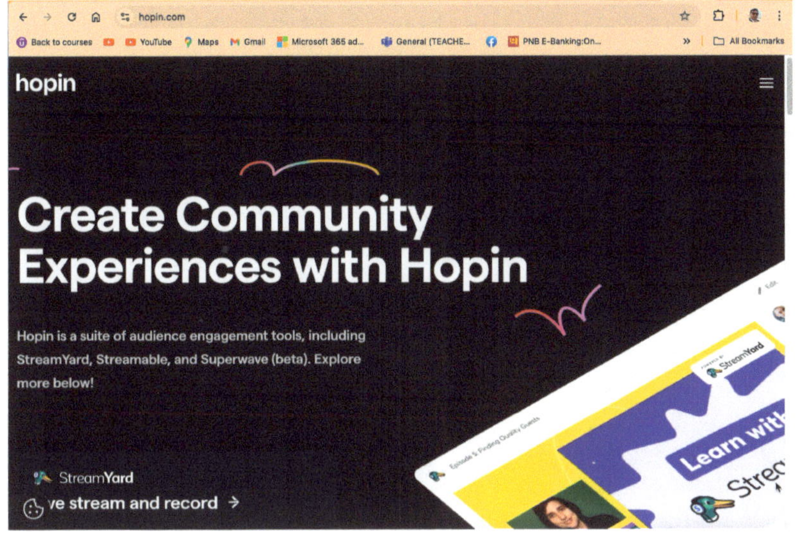

hopin
Create Community
Experiences with Hopin
Hopin is a suite of audience engagement tools, including StreamYard, Streamable, and Superwave (beta). Explore more below!
StreamYard
ve stream and record →
StreamYard
Learn wit
Strea
Episode 5: Finding Quality Guests

www.hopin.com

72. Targeted Content Marketing: Use AI to direct content marketing efforts towards specific parent demographics.

Sample Tool:

Targeted Content Marketing: BrightEdge

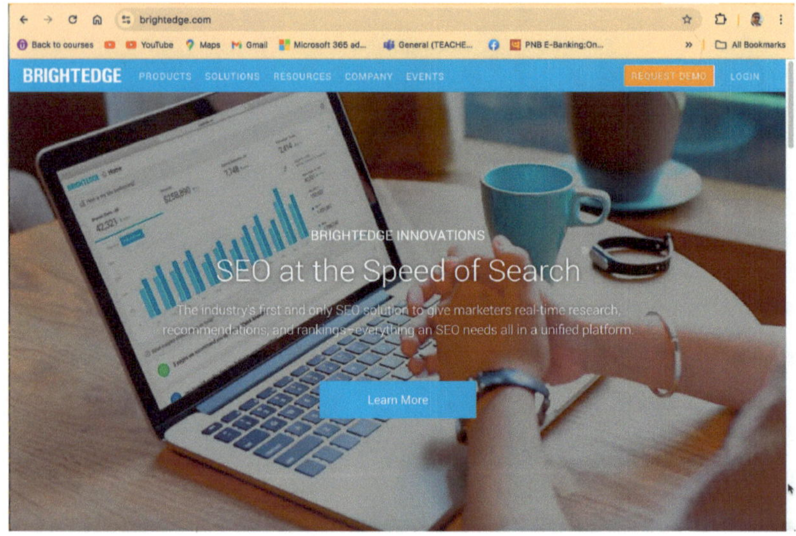
brightedge.com
Back to courses   YouTube   Maps   Gmail   Microsoft 365 ad...   General (TEACHE...   PNB E-Banking:On...   All Bookmarks
BRIGHTEDGE   PRODUCTS   SOLUTIONS   RESOURCES   COMPANY   EVENTS   REQUEST DEMO   LOGIN
BRIGHTEDGE INNOVATIONS
SEO at the Speed of Search
The industry's first and only SEO solution to give marketers real-time research,
recommendations, and rankings - everything an SEO needs all in a unified platform.
Learn More

www.brightedge.com

**73. Predictive Lead Generation: AI can determine
which parents will most enrol their children.**

Sample Tool:

Predictive Lead Generation: Leadspace

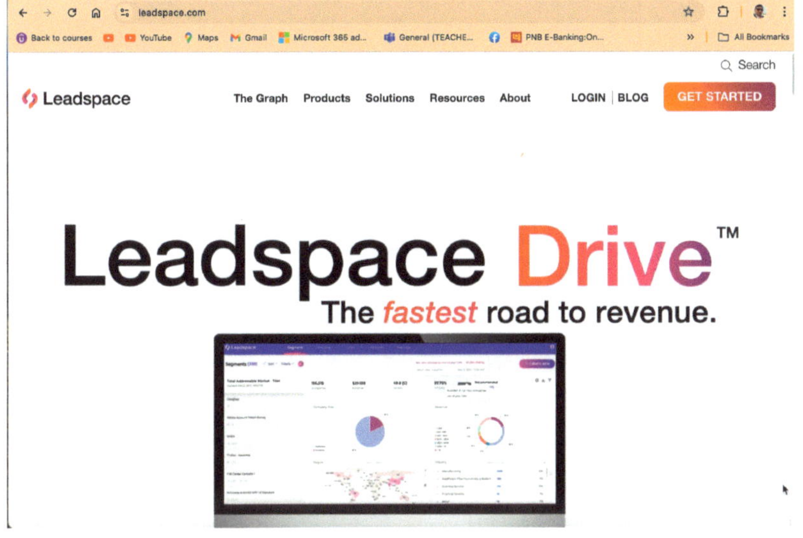

www.leadspace.com

74. Sentiment Analysis for Marketing: Examine parent attitudes towards the school and adjust marketing methods accordingly.

Sample Tool:

Sentiment Analysis for Marketing: Lexalytics

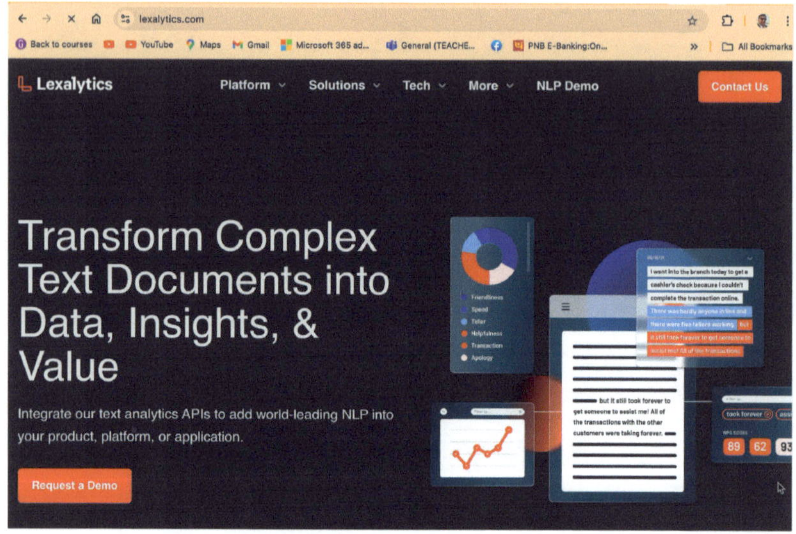
Lexalytics
Platform
Solutions
Tech
More
NLP Demo
Contact Us
Transform Complex
Text Documents into
Data, Insights, &
Value
Integrate our text analytics APIs to add world-leading NLP into
your product, platform, or application.
Request a Demo
Friendliness
Speed
Teller
Helpfulness
Transaction
Apology

www.lexalytics.com

75. AI-Generated Marketing Reports: Utilise AI to provide thorough marketing performance reports.

Sample Tool:

AI-Generated Marketing Reports: Automated Insights

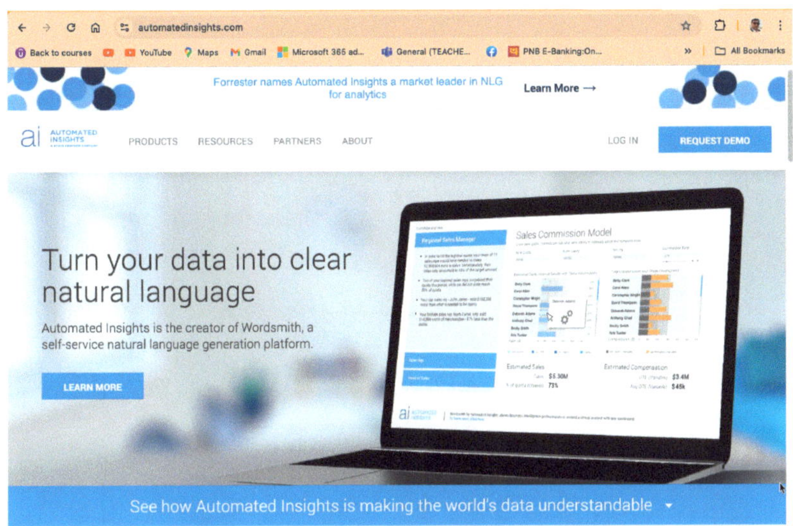

Forrester names Automated Insights a market leader in NLG
for analytics
Learn More →
ai AUTOMATED INSIGHTS
PRODUCTS   RESOURCES   PARTNERS   ABOUT
LOG IN
REQUEST DEMO
Turn your data into clear
natural language
Automated Insights is the creator of Wordsmith, a
self-service natural language generation platform.
LEARN MORE
See how Automated Insights is making the world's data understandable

www.automatedinsights.com

76. Augmented Reality Tours: Provide AI-powered augmented reality tours of the school to prospective parents.

Sample Tool:

Augmented Reality Tours: ThingLink

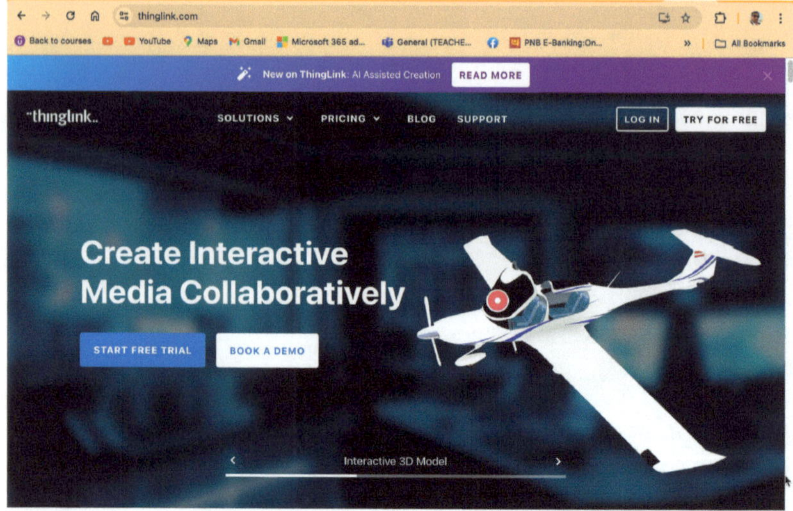

www.thinglink.com

77. AI for Retargeting marketing: Use AI-powered retargeting marketing to keep your school top of mind.

Sample Tool:

AI for Retargeting Marketing: AdRoll

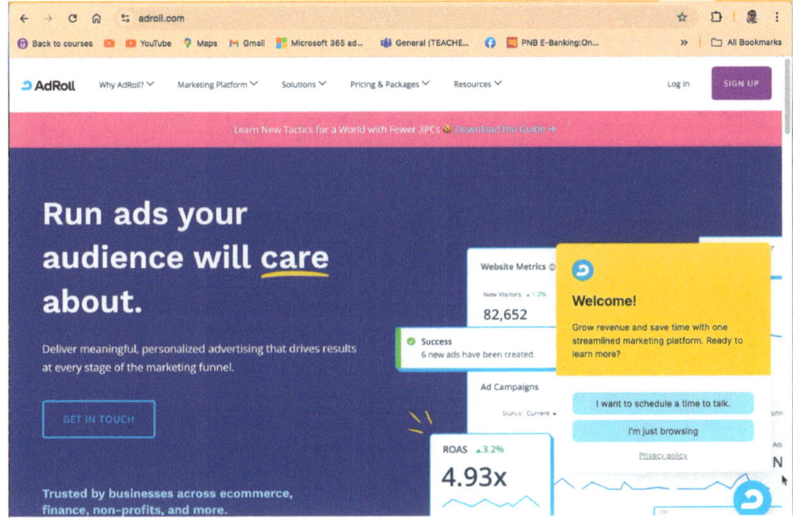
adroll.com
Back to courses   YouTube   Maps   Gmail   Microsoft 365 ad...   General (TEACHE...   PNB E-Banking:On...   All Bookmarks
AdRoll   Why AdRoll?   Marketing Platform   Solutions   Pricing & Packages   Resources   Log in   SIGN UP
Learn New Tactics for a World with Fewer 3PCs   Download the Guide
Run ads your audience will care about.
Deliver meaningful, personalized advertising that drives results at every stage of the marketing funnel.
GET IN TOUCH
Trusted by businesses across ecommerce, finance, non-profits, and more.
Website Metrics
New Visitors   1.2%
82,652
Success
6 new ads have been created.
Ad Campaigns
Status: Current
ROAS   3.2%
4.93x
Welcome!
Grow revenue and save time with one streamlined marketing platform. Ready to learn more?
I want to schedule a time to talk.
I'm just browsing
Privacy policy

www.adroll.com

78. Automated Event Reminders: Use AI to send automated notifications to parents about forthcoming school events.

Sample Tool:

Automated Event Reminders: Zapier with AI

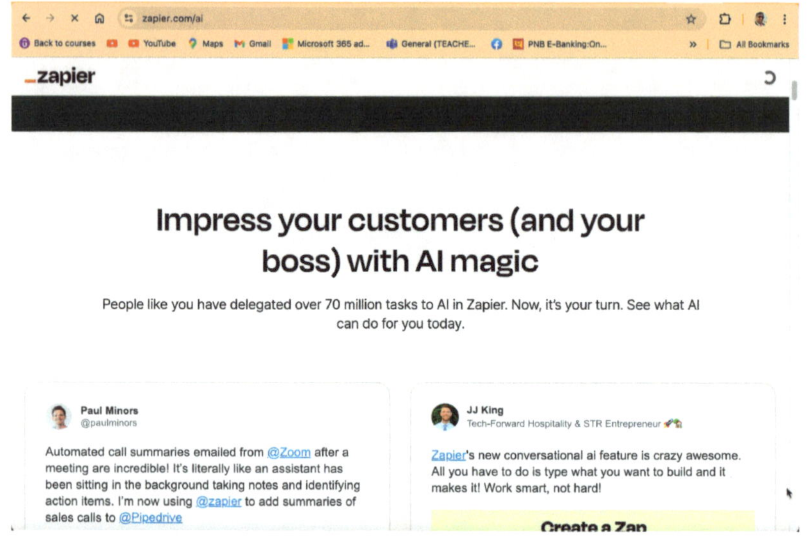
zapier
zapier.com/ai
Back to courses   YouTube   Maps   Gmail   Microsoft 365 ad...   General (TEACHE...   PNB E-Banking:On...   All Bookmarks
Impress your customers (and your boss) with AI magic
People like you have delegated over 70 million tasks to AI in Zapier. Now, it's your turn. See what AI can do for you today.
Paul Minors
@paulminors
Automated call summaries emailed from @Zoom after a meeting are incredible! It's literally like an assistant has been sitting in the background taking notes and identifying action items. I'm now using @zapier to add summaries of sales calls to @Pipedrive
JJ King
Tech-Forward Hospitality & STR Entrepreneur
Zapier's new conversational ai feature is crazy awesome. All you have to do is type what you want to build and it makes it! Work smart, not hard!
Create a Zap

www.zapier.com/ai

79. AI-Enhanced Open Houses: Use AI to personalise open house events.

Sample Tool:

AI-Enhanced Open Houses: Kuula

kuula.co/about
Back to courses   YouTube   Maps   Gmail   Microsoft 365 ad...   General (TEACHE...   PNB E-Banking:On...   All Bookmarks
Explore About Pricing Support Sign-in Register   kuula
kuula
Virtual Tours made easy. Create, edit, share.
Kuula is the most popular virtual tour software to create 3D 360 tours for real estate, architecture, construction, art galleries, education and more.
JOIN NOW!   LEARN MORE
It takes less than 30 seconds!

www.kuula.co/about

80. Data-driven social Media tactics: Use AI to create and improve marketing tactics.

Sample Tool:

Data-driven Social Media Tactics: Sprout Social AI

sproutsocial.com/ai
Back to courses   YouTube   Maps   Gmail   Microsoft 365 ad...   General (TEACHE...   PNB E-Banking:On...   All Bookmarks
sprout social
Platform   Solutions   Pricing   Resources   Log in   Schedule a demo   Try for free
Sprout Social's AI and Automation
Let creativity &
strategic thinking
take center stage
Sprout's AI and automation inherits your manual work in
publishing, listening, analytics, employee advocacy and customer
care so your team can prioritize the decision-making no machine
can emulate.

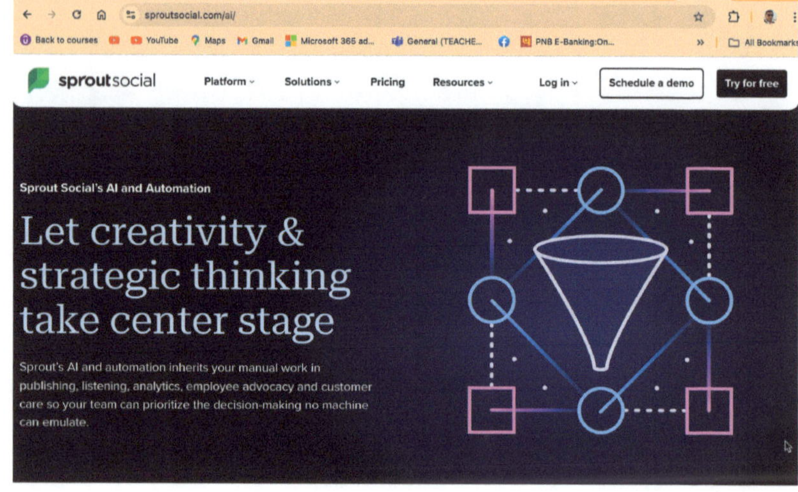

www.sproutsocial.com/ai

**81.   AI-Powered   Interactive   Material: Make
interactive material such as quizzes and polls with
AI.**

Sample Tool:

AI-Powered Interactive Content: Ion Interactive

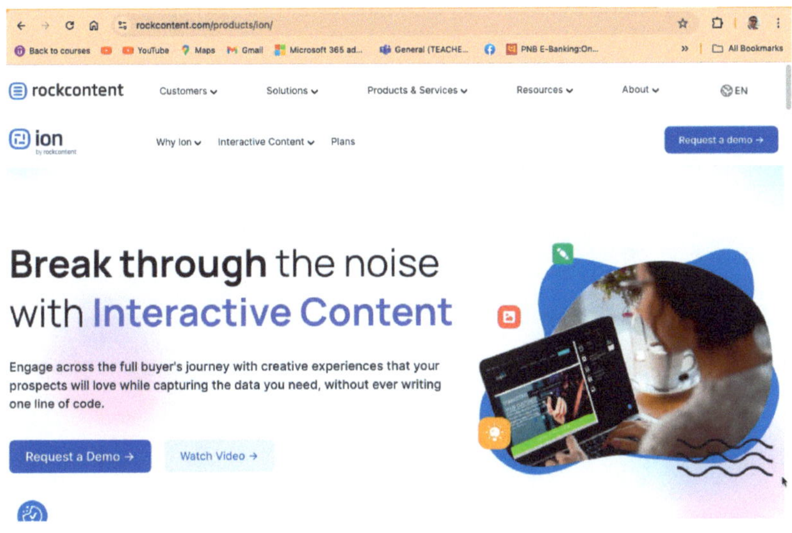
rockcontent.com/products/ion/
Back to courses YouTube Maps Gmail Microsoft 365 ad... General (TEACHE... PNB E-Banking:On... All Bookmarks
rockcontent
Customers
Solutions
Products & Services
Resources
About
EN
ion
by rockcontent
Why Ion
Interactive Content
Plans
Request a demo →
Break through the noise
with Interactive Content
Engage across the full buyer's journey with creative experiences that your
prospects will love while capturing the data you need, without ever writing
one line of code.
Request a Demo →
Watch Video →

www.rockcontent.com

82. AI for Predictive Enrolment Trends: Use artificial intelligence to forecast future enrolment trends and alter marketing efforts accordingly.

Sample Tool:

AI for Predictive Enrollment Trends: Rapid Insight

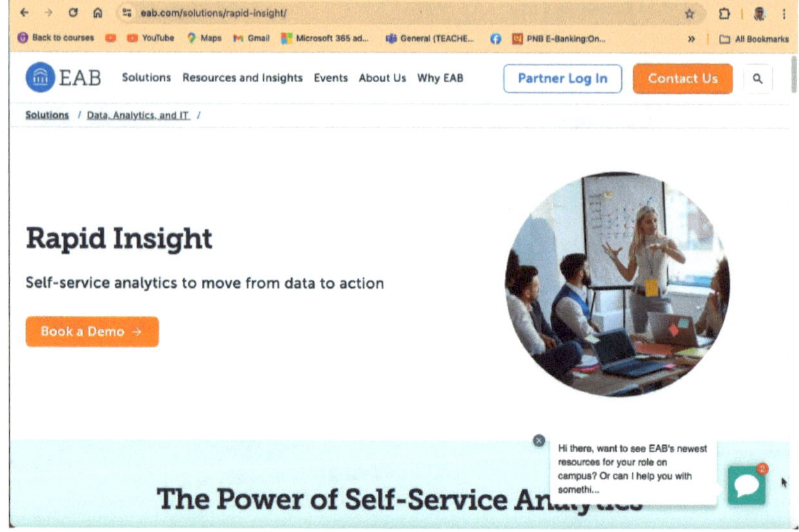

www.eab.com

83. *Interactive Marketing Presentations*: *Use artificial intelligence (AI) to create interactive marketing presentations.*

Sample Tool:

Interactive Marketing Presentations: Beautiful.ai

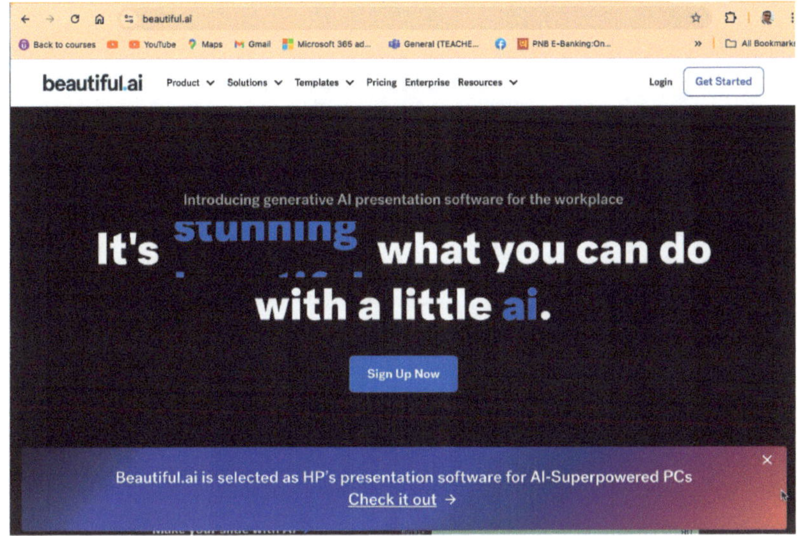
Introducing generative AI presentation software for the workplace
It's stunning what you can do with a little ai.
Sign Up Now
Beautiful.ai is selected as HP's presentation software for AI-Superpowered PCs
Check it out →

www.beautiful.ai

84. AI-Driven Content Personalisation: Use artificial intelligence to personalise website content based on user behaviour.

Sample Tool:

AI-Driven Content Personalization: Optimizely

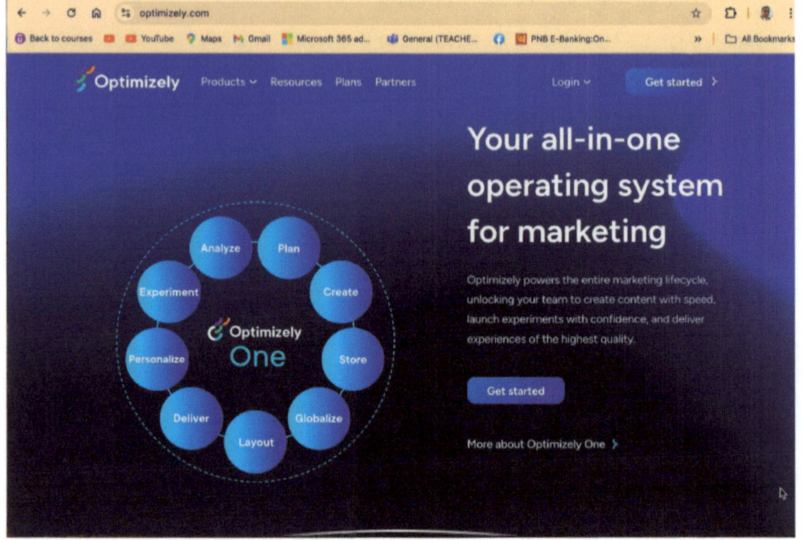
Optimizely
Products Resources Plans Partners
Login
Get started
Your all-in-one operating system for marketing
Optimizely powers the entire marketing lifecycle, unlocking your team to create content with speed, launch experiments with confidence, and deliver experiences of the highest quality.
Get started
More about Optimizely One
Analyze
Plan
Experiment
Create
Optimizely One
Personalize
Store
Deliver
Globalize
Layout

www.optimizely.com

85. Automated Marketing Emails: AI can generate and personalise marketing emails based on parent engagement.

Sample Tool:

Automated Marketing Emails: ActiveCampaign

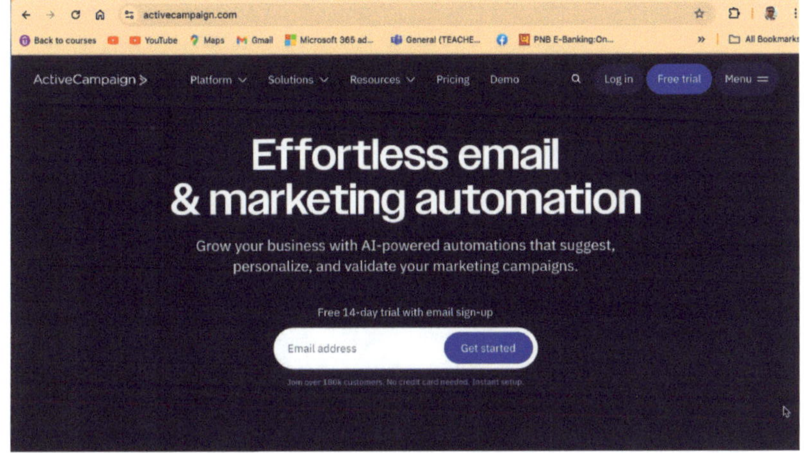
ActiveCampaign
Platform ˅   Solutions ˅   Resources ˅   Pricing   Demo
Log in   Free trial   Menu
Effortless email
& marketing automation
Grow your business with AI-powered automations that suggest,
personalize, and validate your marketing campaigns.
Free 14-day trial with email sign-up
Email address   Get started
Join over 180k customers. No credit card needed. Instant setup.

www.activecampaign.com

86. Smart Social Media Posts: *Use artificial intelligence to schedule and optimise social media posts for optimum engagement.*

Sample Tool:

Smart Social Media Posts: Later with AI

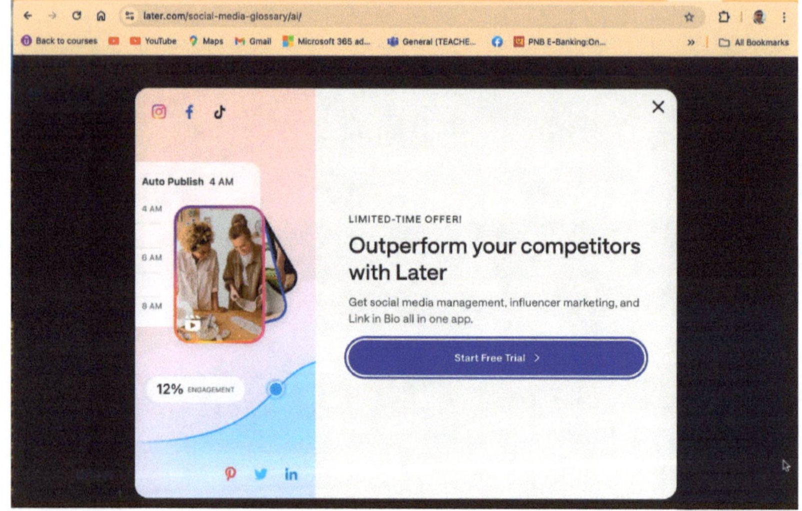

www.later.com/social-media-glossary/ai/

**87. *AI-Driven Parent Outreach: Use AI to discover
and contact potential parents via several channels.***

Sample Tool:

AI-Driven Parent Outreach: Pardot Einstein

Artificial Intelligence
Salesforce Artificial
Intelligence
Salesforce AI delivers trusted, extensible AI grounded
in the fabric of our Einstein 1 Platform. Utilise our AI in
your customer data to create customisable, predictive,
and generative AI experiences to fit all your business
needs safely. Bring conversational AI to any workflow,
user, department, and industry with Einstein.
Talk to an expert
Watch the video
Try for free
Questions?
No problem, we can help. Just start a
chat with one of our sales agents, or
call us at 1800-420-7332.
Let's Chat
No Thanks

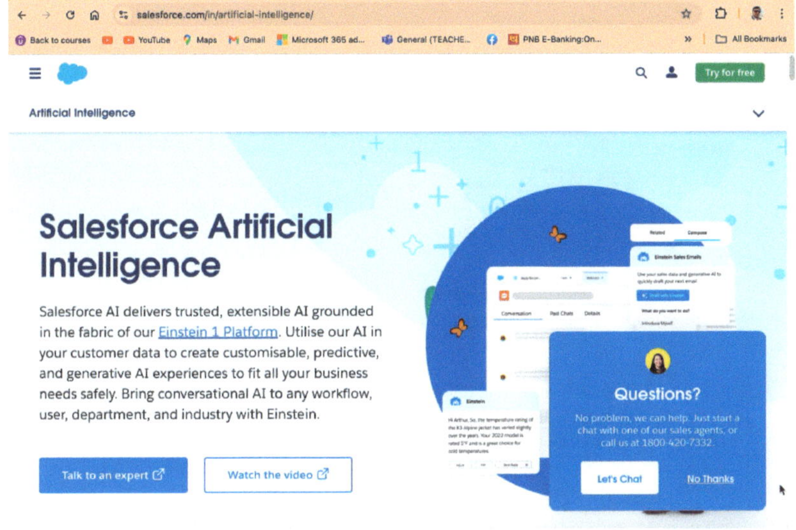

www.salesforce.com/in/artificial-intelligence/

88. Predictive Ad Targeting: AI can forecast the most effective advertising with various parent segments.

Sample Tool:

Predictive Ad Targeting: Adobe Advertising Cloud

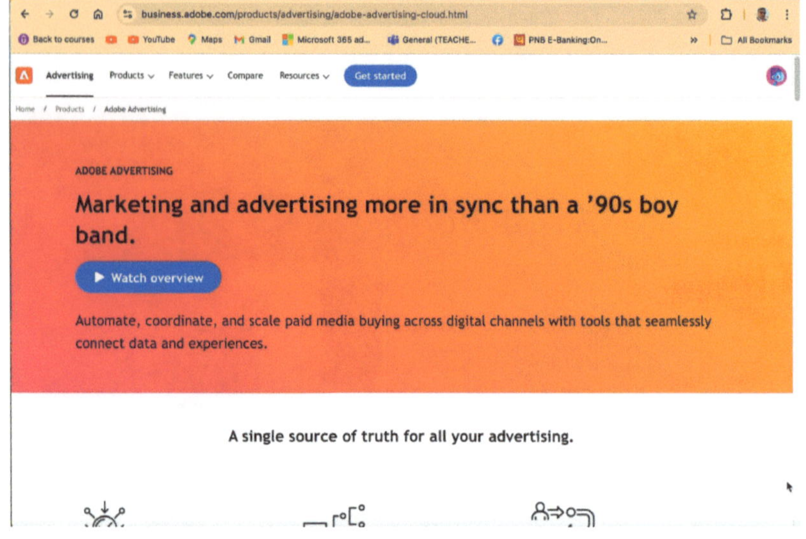
business.adobe.com/products/advertising/adobe-advertising-cloud.html
Back to courses   YouTube   Maps   Gmail   Microsoft 365 ad...   General (TEACHE...   PNB E-Banking:On...   All Bookmarks
Advertising   Products   Features   Compare   Resources   Get started
Home   /   Products   /   Adobe Advertising
ADOBE ADVERTISING
Marketing and advertising more in sync than a '90s boy band.
Watch overview
Automate, coordinate, and scale paid media buying across digital channels with tools that seamlessly connect data and experiences.
A single source of truth for all your advertising.

www.business.adobe.com/products/advertising/adobe-advertising-cloud.html

89. AI-Enhanced School Newsletters: Personalise school newsletters with AI to boost parent involvement.

Sample Tool:

AI-Enhanced School Newsletters: Constant Contact AI

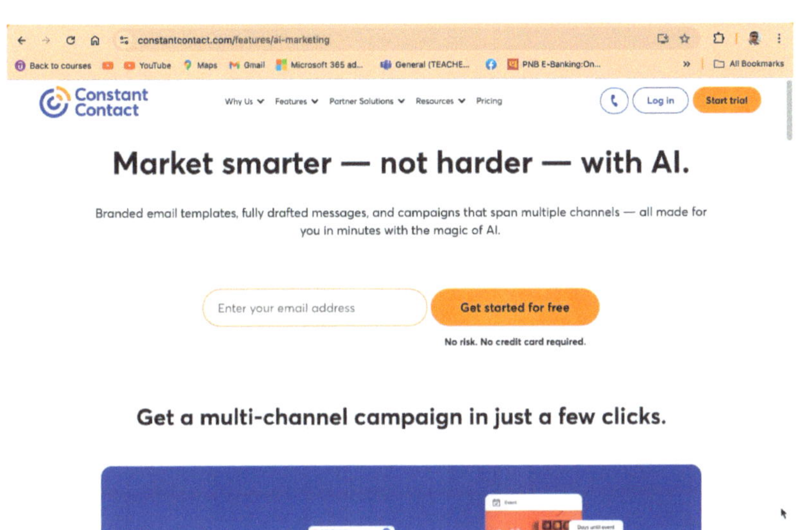
constantcontact.com/features/ai-marketing
Back to courses
YouTube
Maps
Gmail
Microsoft 365 ad...
General (TEACHE...
PNB E-Banking:On...
All Bookmarks
Constant Contact
Why Us
Features
Partner Solutions
Resources
Pricing
Log in
Start trial
Market smarter — not harder — with AI.
Branded email templates, fully drafted messages, and campaigns that span multiple channels — all made for you in minutes with the magic of AI.
Enter your email address
Get started for free
No risk. No credit card required.
Get a multi-channel campaign in just a few clicks.
Bella's
Event
Days until event
3

www.constantcontact.com

90. Dynamic Website Material: Artificial intelligence can provide dynamic website material that varies in response to user interactions.

Sample Tool:

Dynamic Website Content: Acrolinx

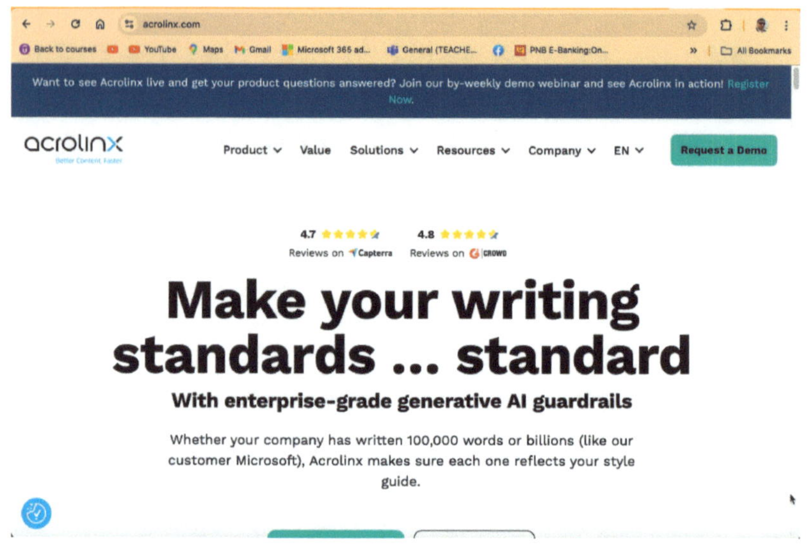
acrolinx.com
Back to courses   YouTube   Maps   Gmail   Microsoft 365 ad...   General (TEACHE...   PNB E-Banking:On...   All Bookmarks
Want to see Acrolinx live and get your product questions answered? Join our by-weekly demo webinar and see Acrolinx in action! Register Now.
acrolinx
Better Content. Faster
Product   Value   Solutions   Resources   Company   EN   Request a Demo
4.7   Reviews on Capterra   4.8   Reviews on CROWD
Make your writing standards ... standard
With enterprise-grade generative AI guardrails
Whether your company has written 100,000 words or billions (like our customer Microsoft), Acrolinx makes sure each one reflects your style guide.

www.acrolinx.com

91. AI for Market Research: Use artificial intelligence (AI) to identify parent preferences and trends.

Sample Tool:

AI for Market Research: Remesh

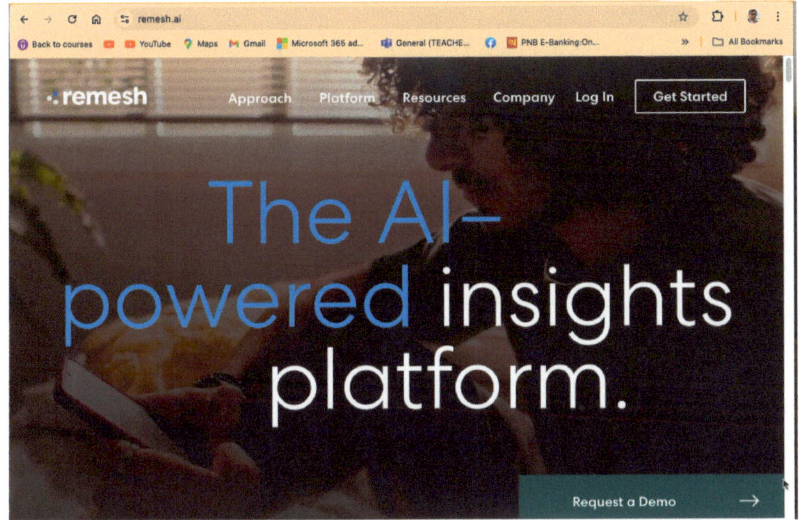

www.remesh.ai

92. AI-Powered Parent Engagement: Use AI to identify and engage less involved parents through personalised outreach.

Sample Tool:

AI-Powered Parent Engagement: Klassly

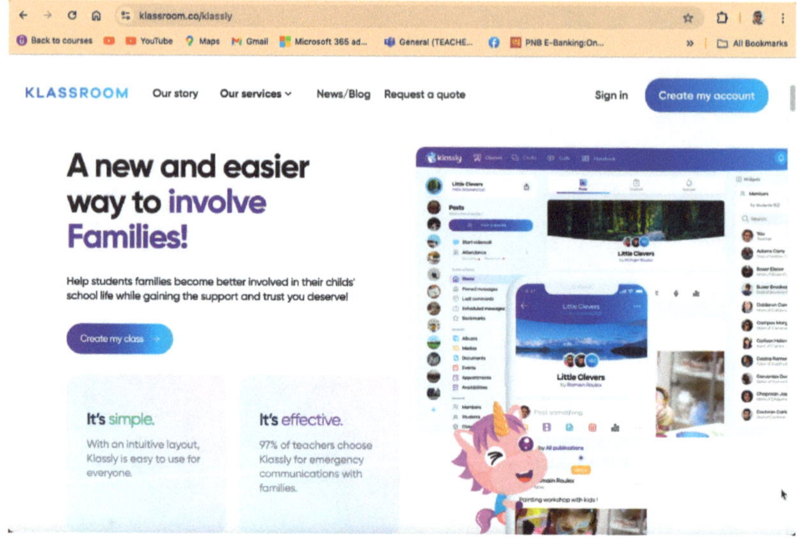
KLASSROOM
Our story   Our services ˅   News/Blog   Request a quote
Sign in   Create my account
A new and easier way to involve Families!
Help students families become better involved in their childs' school life while gaining the support and trust you deserve!
Create my class
It's simple.
With an intuitive layout, Klassly is easy to use for everyone.
It's effective.
97% of teachers choose Klassly for emergency communications with families.

www.klassroom.co/klassly

93. Voice Search Optimisation: Improve the school's Website for AI-powered voice search queries.

Sample Tool:

Voice Search Optimization: BrightEdge

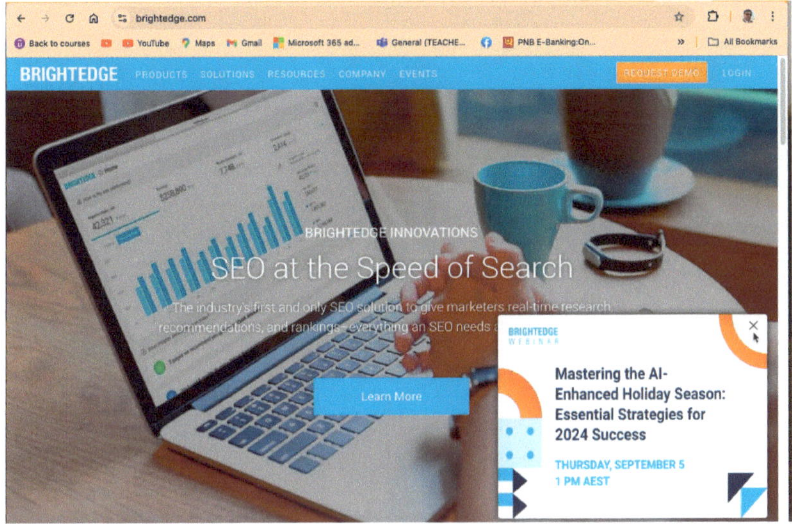

www.brightedge.com

94. AI for Social Proof: Highlight social proof in marketing materials, such as testimonials and reviews.

Sample Tool:

AI for Social Proof: Feefo

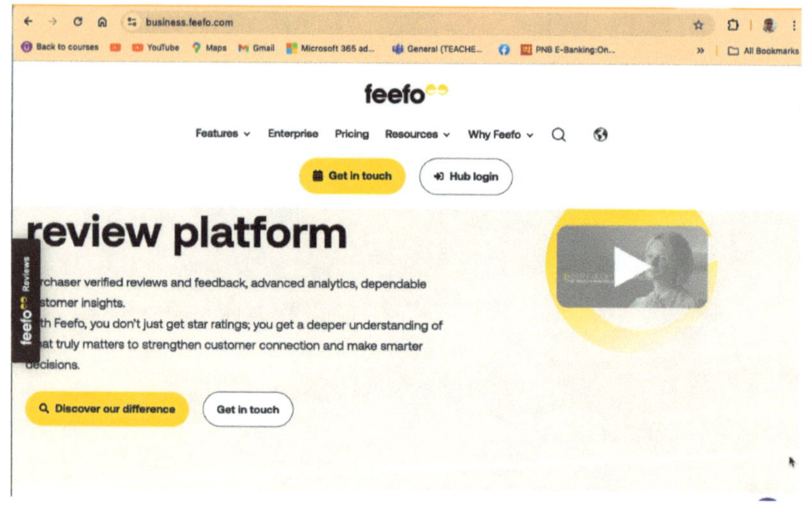
feefo
Features   Enterprise   Pricing   Resources   Why Feefo   Q
Get in touch   Hub login
review platform
rchaser verified reviews and feedback, advanced analytics, dependable
stomer insights.
th Feefo, you don't just get star ratings; you get a deeper understanding of
at truly matters to strengthen customer connection and make smarter
decisions.
Discover our difference   Get in touch

www.business.feefo.com

95. Interactive Marketing Campaigns: *Develop interactive campaigns that engage parents with quizzes and personalised material.*

Sample Tool:

Interactive Marketing Campaigns: SharpSpring

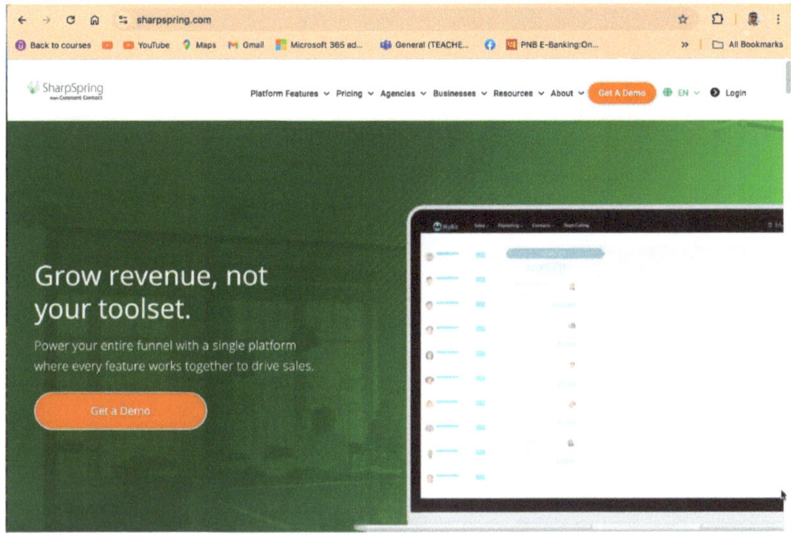

www.sharpspring.com

96. AI-Powered Email Segmentation: Use artificial intelligence to segment email lists based on parental interests.

Sample Tool:

AI-Powered Email Segmentation: Automizy

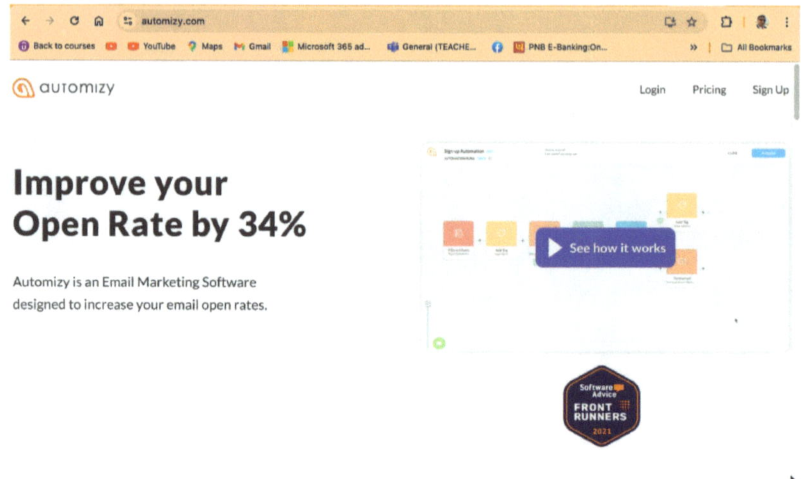
automizy
Login   Pricing   Sign Up
Improve your
Open Rate by 34%
Automizy is an Email Marketing Software
designed to increase your email open rates.
See how it works
Software Advice
FRONT RUNNERS
2021

www.automizy.com

97. Automated Social Media Ads: *Use artificial intelligence to automatically create and place social media advertisements.*

Sample Tool:

Automated Social Media Ads: Smartly.io

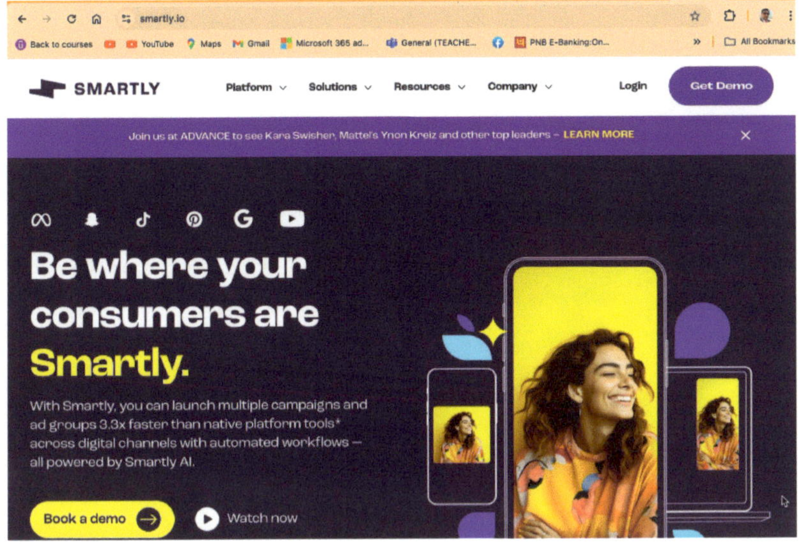
smartly.io
Back to courses   YouTube   Maps   Gmail   Microsoft 365 ad...   General (TEACHE...   PNB E-Banking:On...   All Bookmarks
SMARTLY
Platform   Solutions   Resources   Company   Login   Get Demo
Join us at ADVANCE to see Kara Swisher, Mattel's Ynon Kreiz and other top leaders – LEARN MORE
Be where your consumers are
Smartly.
With Smartly, you can launch multiple campaigns and ad groups 3.3x faster than native platform tools* across digital channels with automated workflows — all powered by Smartly AI.
Book a demo
Watch now

www.smartly.io

98. AI-Generated Social Media Content: Use artificial intelligence to create social media content that parents will appreciate.

Sample Tool:

AI-Generated Social Media Content: Lately

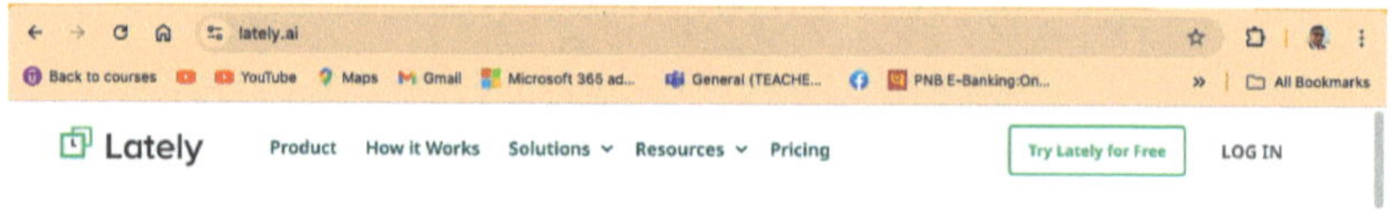

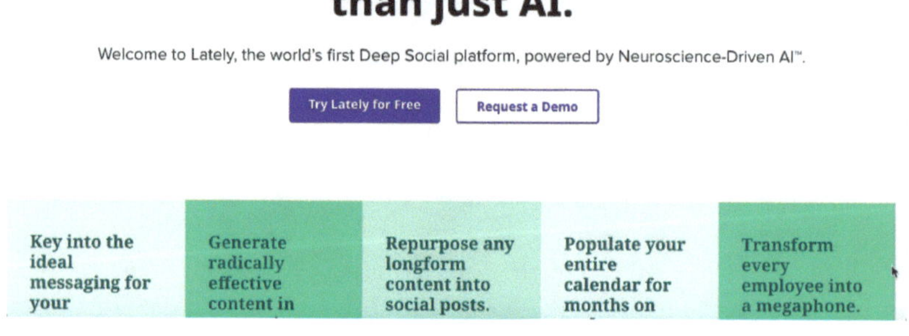
Revolutionize your social with more than just AI.
Welcome to Lately, the world's first Deep Social platform, powered by Neuroscience-Driven AI™.
Try Lately for Free
Request a Demo
Key into the ideal messaging for your
Generate radically effective content in
Repurpose any longform content into social posts.
Populate your entire calendar for months on
Transform every employee into a megaphone.

www.lately.ai

99. AI for Competitive Analysis: Using AI, analyse competitors' efforts to improve the school's marketing approach.

Sample Tool:

AI for Competitive Analysis: Kompyte

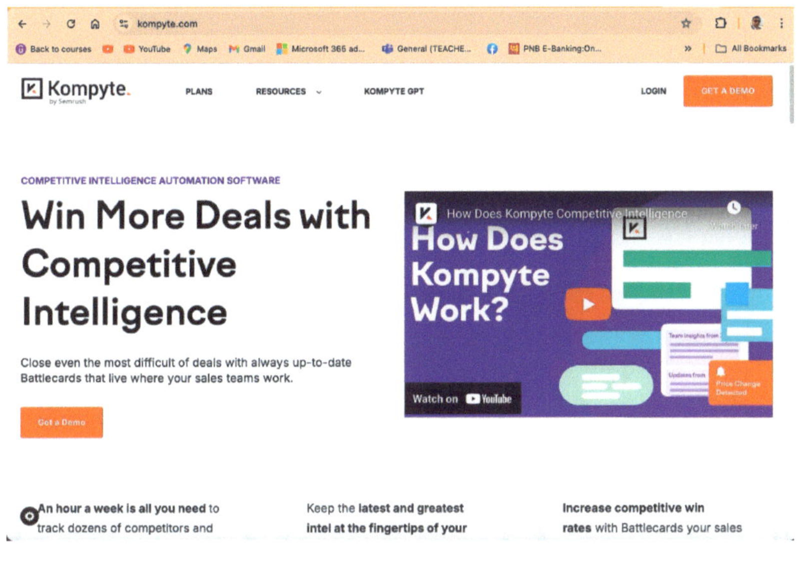
kompyte.com
Back to courses   YouTube   Maps   Gmail   Microsoft 365 ad...   General (TEACHE...   PNB E-Banking:On...   All Bookmarks
Kompyte.
by Semrush
PLANS   RESOURCES   KOMPYTE GPT   LOGIN   GET A DEMO
COMPETITIVE INTELLIGENCE AUTOMATION SOFTWARE
Win More Deals with Competitive Intelligence
Close even the most difficult of deals with always up-to-date Battlecards that live where your sales teams work.
Get a Demo
How Does Kompyte Competitive Intelligence
How Does Kompyte Work?
Watch on YouTube
An hour a week is all you need to track dozens of competitors and
Keep the latest and greatest intel at the fingertips of your
Increase competitive win rates with Battlecards your sales

www.kompyte.com

100. AI-Driven Parent Engagement: Use AI to identify and engage parents not actively engaging in school activities.

Sample Tool:

AI-Driven Parent Engagement: ParentSquare AI

parentsquare.com
Back to courses   YouTube   Maps   Gmail   Microsoft 365 ad...   General (TEACHE...   PNB E-Banking:On...   All Bookmarks
Ready, set, go! Start your year off strong with the Back-to-School Checklist for School-Home Communications
ParentSquare   Product   Resources   Company   Blog   Get a Demo   Sign In
Build Stronger Connections With Families
Everything you need to communicate, involve and collaborate with families for student success
Get a Demo

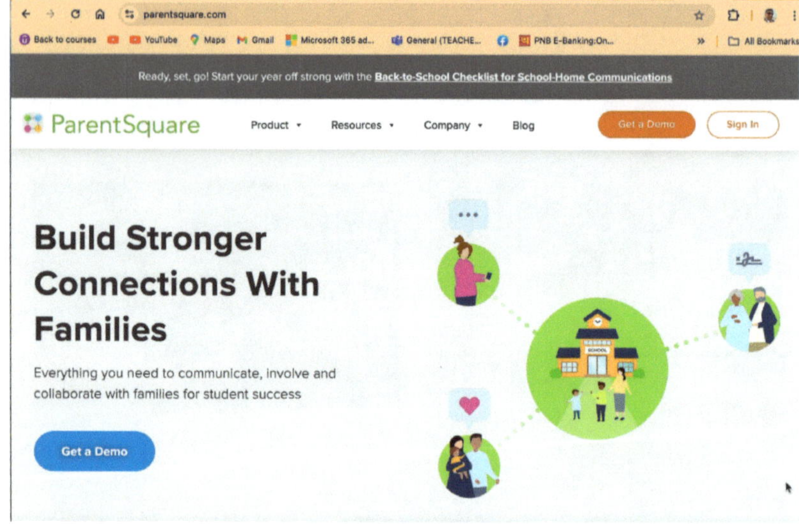

www.parentsquare.com

These techniques can significantly increase a school's visibility, reputation, and enrolment by exploiting AI's capabilities.

TWO
BOOKS BY THE SAME AUTHOR

101
SCHOOL
MANAGEMENT
STRATEGIES
Towards EFFECTIVE
QUALITY MANAGEMENT
System in Schools
DR. DHEERAJ
MEHROTRA

ORDER
ONLINE

SECURING SAFETY & QUALITY CARING
99 SAFETY AND
SECURITY
ANCHORS WITHIN SCHOOLS
DR. DHEERAJ MEHROTRA
A
PRIORITY
FOR
SCHOOLS
www.authordheerajmehrotra.com

THREE

About The Author

Dheeraj Mehrotra, MS, MPhil, PhD (Education Management)., a white and a yellow belt in SIX SIGMA, a Certified NLP Business Diploma holder, is an Educational Innovator, Author, with expertise in Six Sigma In Education, Academic Audits, Neuro-Linguistic Programming (NLP), Total Quality Management In Education, an Experiential Educator, a CBSE Resource towards School Assessment (SQAA), CCE, JIT, Five S, and KAIZEN. He has authored over 100 books on computer science, AI, digital body language, NLP, quality circles, school management, classroom effectiveness, and safety and security. A former Principal at De Indian Public School, New Delhi, (INDIA), NPS International School, Guwahati, and Education Officer at GEMS, Gurgaon, with ample teaching experience of over Three Decades, he is a certified Trainer for Quality Circles/ TQM in Education and QCI Standards for School Accreditation/ School Audits and Management. He has also been honoured with the President of India's National Teacher Award in 2006 and the Best Science Teacher State Award (By the Ministry of Science and Technology, State of UP), Innovation in Education for his inception of Six Sigma In Education by Education Watch, New Delhi and Education World- Best Teacher Award, BOLT Learner Teacher Award by Air India, 'Innovation in Education Award 2016' by Higher Education Forum (HEF), Gujarat Chapter, among others. He has developed over 150 FREE EDUCATIONAL MOBILE Apps for the Google Play Store exclusively for Teachers, Students, and Parents. This work has been recognised by the LIMCA BOOK OF RECORDS and INDIA BOOK OF RECORDS as the only Indian to draw that feast. As a founder president of the IoT Society of India, he also promotes Technology Globally. Dr Mehrotra is presently engaged as a PRINCIPAL at KUNWARS GLOBAL SCHOOL, Lucknow, India. He has conducted over 2000 workshops globally on "Excellence In Education" integrated with Total Quality Management and Six Sigma, Technology Integration in Education (TIE), Developing towards being ROCKSTAR TEACHERS, including Cyberspace, Cyber Security, Classroom Management, School Leadership & Management, and Innovative teaching within classrooms via Mind Maps, NLP and Experiential Learning in Academics. He is an active TEDx speaker and can be viewed on the YouTube TEDx channel. As a premium UDEMY Instructor, he has developed over 500 courses and caters to over 8 Lakh students from 180 countries. He can be visited at www.authordheerajmehrotra.com